NURSE PRESC

Nurse Prescribing

Second Edition

Edited by

Jennifer L. Humphries

and

Joyce Green

WITH A FOREWORD BY
BARONESS CUMBERLEGE

palgrave

First edition 1999
Reprinted three times
Second edition published 2002 by
PALGRAVE
Houndmills, Basingstoke, Hampshire RG21 6XS and
175 Fifth Avenue, New York, N.Y. 10010
Companies and representatives throughout the world

PALGRAVE is the new global academic imprint of
St. Martin's Press LLC Scholarly and Reference Division and
Palgrave Publishers Ltd (formerly Macmillan Press Ltd).

ISBN 0–333–93092–4 paperback

This book is printed on paper suitable for recycling and made from fully managed and sustained forest sources.

A catalogue record for this book is available from the British Library.

10   9   8   7   6   5   4
11 10 09 08 07 06 05 04

Editing and origination by
Aardvark Editorial, Mendham, Suffolk

Printed in Great Britain by
J.W. Arrowsmith, Bristol

To Steve, Tristram and Geraint

Publisher's note

The publisher and the authors make no representation, express or implied, with regard to the accuracy of the information contained in this book and cannot accept any legal responsibility or liability for any errors or omissions.

This work is intended as an overview of the field and while it is, to the best of the editors' knowledge, correct at the time of writing, the editors, contributors and publisher shall have no liability for its use as a basis for clinical practice or legal action in respect of which independent professional advice should be sought in relation to specific circumstance.

Contents

Notes on contributors

Rosalyn Anderson BSc(Hons), DipTherMR, PharmS

Independent Pharmaceutical Adviser, Lorac Clinical Pharmacy Services, Cheadle, Cheshire

Ros is a pharmacist who undertakes prescribing reviews within primary care for GPs and community and practice nurses. She works jointly with nurse practitioners on anticoagulant and medication review clinics, was involved in training nurse prescribers from the initial pilot work in Bolton and subsequently, and has analysed nurse prescribing data for the Department of Health. She has also lectured to health professionals on many aspects of prescribing, including wound care, incontinence and stoma products, and has written bulletins on these topics for the National Prescribing Centre.

Mark Campbell MPhil, MRPharmS

Pharmaceutical Adviser, Bury and Rochdale Health Authority

Mark is responsible for strategic advice to the health authority and its primary care organisations on all prescribing and medicines management issues. He has been teaching nurse prescribers for eight years and has recently been appointed a National Prescribing Centre training adviser.

Joyce Green MA, BA, RN, RM, RHV, QN, NDNCert, RNT, DNT

Joyce was involved with community nurse education for many years and has been a course leader for both district nursing and practice nursing and joint course leader for the nurse prescribing course. She was a member of the ENB Nurse Prescribing Steering Group and a member of the ENB Working Group (1997/98) which revised the *Nurse Prescribing: Open Learning Pack*. Joyce was involved in developing and delivering the nurse prescribing course at Manchester Metropolitan University and in satelliting the approved course to seven other institutions in the third phase of the introduction of nurse prescribing. Since her retirement, Joyce has continued to maintain her interest and involvement with nurse prescribing, including acting as external examiner for nurse prescribing courses at two universities.

Eileen Groves MA (Health Care Ethics), RN, DN, DNT, RNT, CertEd

Senior Lecturer, Department of Health Care Studies, Manchester Metropolitan University

Eileen has a background in community nursing and community nurse education, having been a course tutor for district nursing for many years. She is currently course leader to the nurse prescribing course and lecturer in health care ethics and law. Eileen is also a member of a local research ethics committee and a PCG board member.

Jennifer L. Humphries MA, BSc(Hons), RN, RM, RHV, RHVT, CertEd, DipHE (School Nursing)

Senior Lecturer, Department of Primary and Community Nursing, University of Central Lancashire

Jennifer has been teaching in community nurse education since 1990 and has been a lecturer/module leader for nurse prescribing since 1994. She was involved in developing and delivering the pilot nurse prescribing course and, with Joyce Green, participated in satelliting the approved course at Manchester Metropolitan University to other institutions in the third phase of the introduction of nurse prescribing. Jennifer served as a consultant in the development of the prescribing bulletins and educational material produced by the National Prescribing Centre. She is currently leading the nurse prescribing course at the University of Central Lancashire and is an active researcher in this aspect of nursing practice.

Rita Hurst SRN, NDNCert

District Nursing Sister/Practice Nurse, Community Healthcare, Bolton NHS Trust

Rita was a district nurse for 17 years. She became one of the first community nurses in the country to prescribe when the GP practice she worked with was chosen as one of the eight pilot sites in 1994. She has addressed many conferences and is an experienced speaker on the subject of nurse prescribing. She was part of the ENB Working Group (1997/98) revising the *Nurse Prescribing: Open Learning Pack*. She is currrently working as a practice nurse in Bolton.

Lorraine Lowe (née Berry) RGN, DipHV, MA

Health Visitor/Nurse Practitioner, Community Healthcare, Bolton NHS Trust

Lorraine qualified as a health visitor at the same time as the pilot for nurse prescribing commenced in Bolton. As an experienced nurse prescriber, she has addressed many conferences on the subject. She has participated in the nurse prescribing course at Manchester Metropolitan University by sharing her skills and experiences with student nurse prescribers. She works with a GP practice in a dual role as health visitor and nurse practitioner, and also works as freelance nurse adviser in respiratory care with several primary care practices.

Steven Preece BA(HONS), CERTED, SOLICITOR
Partner, Health Department, Hill Dickinson Solicitors, Liverpool

Steven acts on behalf of Health Authorities and Trusts in the North West of England, the North Midlands and North Wales, dealing mainly with clinical negligence claims, but he also advises on a wide range of legal issues relating to health care generally. He has a particular interest in the law in relation to health professionals' practice and is the legal adviser to the Association for Nurse Prescribing. Steven lectures widely on legal issues relating to health care and is a visiting lecturer at a number of universities. He is a member of the Court of the University of Liverpool, the Liverpool Research Ethics Committee and the advisory board of a hospice on Merseyside.

Joel Richman BA, MA(ECON), PHD

Joel is a founder member of Manchester Polytechnic, now the Manchester Metropolitan University. Publications include: *Traffic Wardens: An Ethnography of Street Administration* (Manchester University Press 1983), *Medicine and Health* (Longman 1987) and *Health* (Macmillan 1992 – now Palgrave)). He has made contributions to several edited books and journals. Before retirement, Joel was awarded a chair in medical sociology and anthropology. As emeritus professor, he continues to work part time in the Department of Health Care Studies at Manchester Metropolitan University.

David Skidmore MSc, PHD, RN, DIPN, CERTED, DIPPE
Head of Department of Health Care Studies, Manchester Metropolitan University

David was a community psychiatric nurse and behavioural therapist in the early 1970s prior to taking up full-time study in medical sociology. He subsequently fell into an academic career and has been involved with community nursing research for some 25 years. His interest in the education and development of nursing practice had its genesis in community research in the 1980s, and he has been actively involved in this field of research ever since.

Foreword to the first edition

In 1986 I started what was to become the long haul to allow nurses to prescribe. It seemed logical, sensible and fairly easy to achieve. A survey of community nurses conducted in 1985 showed that 30 per cent cleaned the surgery and for GPs the most important job of the nurse was to fill his or her bag. Nurse prescribing became a giant cultural hurdle to turn handmaidens into autonomous practitioners.

While there was enthusiasm for the project from many nurses and doctors, others found the change difficult, not least the Treasury, many politicians and parts of the NHS establishment. It was part of the feminist revolution which was being fought in every walk of life from the Church of England to cricket clubs. Nurse prescribing triggered a wholesale reassessment of the role of nurses, their training and the move to a profession qualified with degrees in nursing.

The transition has not been easy; long delays, primary legislation and dealing with the implications for nearly half a million nurses. We are now at the stage where all community nurses are or will soon be able to prescribe, and the move towards enabling all specialist nurses to take that responsibility is unstoppable.

It is a quiet, continuing revolution which must not lose its momentum, because it not only strengthens teamwork but does so much to improve the health care to all the people of this country.

BARONESS CUMBERLEGE

Foreword to the second edition

If you have ever felt small, insignificant or unable to make your mark, you have never been to bed with a mosquito!

For decades nurses have struggled to ensure their skills and ability are not overlooked and their professional role is recognised. For my part, I have fought to ensure they have the tools so necessary to fulfil their role. Part of this fight has been to see the introduction of nurse prescribing.

Successive governments have been reluctant to allow nurses to make clinical judgements in terms of prescribing, but every year we get a little closer to allowing all nurses to prescribe and to have the full rein of the *Formulary* – although there is still some way to go.

With constant and rapid change in the structure of the NHS it is crucial not to let past achievements fade. My concern is that the new primary care teams, strategic health authorities and workforce confederations will not put into nurse prescribing the investment which is so essential.

A worse fear is that nurses will not take advantage of the enormous opportunities open to them. Already there is evidence that some nurses with the necessary qualifications and training lack the confidence to prescribe. This is really tragic – tragic for the nursing profession and tragic for patients. When pain, suffering and discomfort can be alleviated, surely a true professional can summon up the confidence to prescribe the necessary treatment?

I do not want to ignore the important issue of safety, and of course that is of paramount importance, but neither do I want nurses to ignore the opportunities they have to do the best for patients in their care. That is why this excellent and comprehensive book is so important. It will help to instil the confidence which is so necessary for every nurse prescriber.

Congratulations to Jennifer Humphries and Joyce Green for updating *Nurse Prescribing*. The initial edition was appreciated and much used but, instead of resting on their laurels, they have tackled the task again and brought it up to date. I hope it will be widely used and appreciated, and go far in ensuring better care for patients.

BARONESS CUMBERLEGE

Preface

Nurse prescribing is an innovative project in the UK. It has government support but its progress has been relatively slow; the idea of nurses prescribing was first put forward in 1986 yet when the first edition of this book was published in 1999, prescribing by nurses was restricted to district nurses and health visitors who had undergone specialised training. Since that time the development of nurse prescribing has gained momentum, largely due to the success of the initiative for which the original nurse prescribers should take credit. The expansion of the *Nurse Prescribers' Formulary* and the extension to a wider range of nurses of the authority to prescribe are welcome. It means that many more nurses, working in a variety of roles and settings, will now be able to prescribe products for their patients and clients.

Nurse Prescribing proved to be a crucial text for students on nurse prescribing courses and we are grateful to those nurses and health visitors who thanked us for the book. Their comments and those of other readers, the reviews of the first edition, and our own continuing experience of nurse prescribing have led to a second, significantly updated, edition. The major aim is unaltered from the original, that is, to provide access to a range of perspectives on nurse prescribing and to promote discourse on these issues. The book takes a critical look at the development and implications of nurse prescribing, discussing features relating to patients and clients, the nurses themselves and the nursing profession in general. Relevant professional issues are examined and comprehensively reviewed within the framework of current nursing practice. The chapters have been written by different authors and, because of this, readers may perceive variations in style and presentation of material. It has not been our intention to edit out these differences, as each contributor has his or her own unique body of knowledge and expertise to add to the nurse prescribing discussion. By offering a range of perspectives, this will enrich the content, enabling readers, whether current prescribers or not, to consider prescribing in the context of their professional role and to reflect on the implications from both local and national perspectives.

Chapter 1 sets the scene by presenting a historical overview of the nurse prescribing initiative within a legislative framework, outlining the development of the training programme and indicating how nurse prescribing fits in with contemporary nursing practice. It has been updated to bring nurse prescribing up to the present time.

Chapter 2 covers the very important issues of ethical principles and accountability. It has been extensively developed from the first edition so much so that a separate chapter was deemed necessary, signifying the vital part that the ethical dimension plays in nurse prescribing. The incorporation of case studies, that will stimulate thought and discussion, is an added element that takes account of the usefulness of this approach.

The importance of the legal issues that surround nurse prescribing compelled us to consider that they too required a separate chapter. Thus Chapter 3 looks comprehensively at the legal perspective of nurse prescribing and the aspects of nurses' accountability in relation to this.

In Chapter 4 assessment and evaluation strategies are discussed in some detail and the arguments presented clearly demonstrate how these strategies are applied to nurse prescribing and assist nurses in the decision-making process.

Chapter 5 offers a rich source of practical information on the responsibilities of prescribing including guidance for prescription writing, generic prescribing and independent reference sources for prescribers.

Chapter 6 discusses some of the financial implications of prescribing and the ways in which nurse prescribing is being monitored. Some national and international perspectives are also considered.

Chapter 7 focuses on concordance, non-compliance and who is the non-compliant patient. A review of the extensive research in this area, although naturally medically based, has much to offer prescribing nurses and will increase awareness and stimulate debate.

The reality of nurse prescribing is illustrated in Chapter 8 through the experiences of nurses who have been prescribing since participating in the demonstration project in 1994. Case examples of prescribing situations are included, focusing the reader on some of the pertinent issues that nurse prescribing raises and enabling reflection on current practice.

Chapter 9 takes a considered look at the extended role of the nurse by analysing the role of specialist practitioners and putting nurse prescribing as the central focus of this debate. This poses many questions about which nurses should be able to prescribe, how far the nurse's role should progress, the benefits for patients/clients and the implications for the nursing profession. The intention is to provoke the reader to take a critical look at nursing and the possible implications of extending the scope of clinical practice.

Chapter 10 is a completely new chapter that again takes account of the comments from readers of the original book and our experiences in working with nurse prescribing students. This chapter is devoted to considering case studies that allow readers to examine the range of issues that can occur, from the moral and ethical dimension through to the practical aspects of prescribing (or not) products.

The book concludes, in Chapter 11, with an examination of the most recent developments that have occurred in the sphere of nurse prescribing. It looks at current issues and considers some possible future implications for nursing practice.

The nurse prescribing initiative is a changing one but, as emphasised in *Making a Difference* (DoH 1999), it is here to stay. The text is an edited compilation of practical and theoretical perspectives relating to nurse prescribing, supported by reference to relevant reading and research. However the book also offers a no-nonsense and jargon-free approach. Comments about the first edition frequently noted the essential 'readability' of the book, a feature that we have strived to maintain. We are indebted to the contributors who shared our vision that the book should continue to be interesting and informative but, significantly, enjoyable to the readers. We hope that we have achieved our objective.

Although aimed primarily at nurses and a necessary text for all those undertaking a nurse prescribing course, by adopting a broad approach to nurse prescribing, the intention is to appeal to all health care professionals. The book will also be useful to nurses who are already prescribers or who supply and administer medications by way of patient group directions. Nurse prescribing is a momentous evolution in nursing practice, and we consider this book to be essential supplementary reading for both student nurses and those undertaking any post-registration courses. The

Scope of Professional Practice (UKCC 1992) outlines the need for practice and education to be sensitive, relevant and responsive to the changing needs of patients and clients. Nurse prescribing is one such initiative and it behoves all nurses and health care professionals to be aware of contemporary issues affecting nursing practice and patient/client care.

References

DoH (1999) *Making a Difference*. DoH, London.
UKCC (1992) *Scope of Professional Practice*. UKCC, London.

Development of the nurse prescribing initiative

Joyce Green

Nurse prescribing is a comparatively new and exciting development for the nursing profession, the vision of community nurses
and health visitors being able to prescribe for patients having
begun in 1986. This chapter will incorporate a historical overview
of the nurse prescribing initiative and include reference to relevant reports and legislation, a brief summary of the pilot sites and
how the training for nurse prescribing developed. Issues relating
to teamwork in primary health care, including community
profiling and case load management, and circumstances in which
a nurse may prescribe, will be addressed in order to illustrate how
nurse prescribing fits in with the current role of nursing practice.

A historical overview of the legislative framework

According to Blatt (1997), nurse prescribing is not a new idea but
was first recommended by the Royal College of Nursing (RCN)
in 1980, and became part of the government's policy agenda in
1986 with the Cumberlege Report. A team, chaired by Julia
Cumberlege, was appointed in June 1985, its terms of reference
in the frontispiece being:

> To study the nursing services provided outside hospital by Health Authorities,
> and to report to the Secretary of State on how resources can be used more
> effectively, so as to improve the services available to client groups. The input
> from nurses employed by general practitioners will be taken into account.
>
> (DHSS 1986)

The Review Team were asked to report to the Secretary of
State by the end of the year so had six months in which to gather
and collate their evidence. During this period, district nurses

indicated that, based on a full nursing assessment of the patients' individual health care needs, they were constantly recommending to general practitioners (GPs) the need for particular dressings or appliances for patients. However, they had to get the GPs to sanction and sign the prescriptions, which was felt to be very time wasting. In addition, according to Cumberlege (DHSS 1986), many nurses had also become very skilled in managing pain relief for terminally ill patients.

The following recommendation was included in the Report:

> that the DHSS should agree a limited list of items and simple agents which may be prescribed by nurses as part of a nursing care programme, and issue guidelines to enable nurses to control drug dosage in well-defined circumstances.
>
> (DHSS 1986, p. 33)

This recommendation and its implications were subsequently reviewed by the Department of Health (DoH) advisory group chaired by Dr June Crown.

The Crown Report, published in 1989 (DoH 1989), recommended that suitably qualified nurses working in the community, defined as those nurses with a district nurse or health visitor qualification, should be authorised to prescribe in defined circumstances from a limited list of items to be included in the *Nurse Prescribers' Formulary* (NPF) (see Appendix 1). They also recommended that nurses should be able to supply medicines within group protocols or adjust their timing and dosage within patient-specific protocols. These protocol issues were not taken further at that time which, according to Jones and Gough (1997), was viewed 'as a lost opportunity'.

Subsequently, Mr Roger Simms, Member of Parliament for Chislehurst, introduced a Private Member's Bill making legislative provision for nurse prescribing; this received Royal Assent in March 1992. Since then, much work has been undertaken in order to ensure that nurse prescribing is implemented in an efficient and cost-effective way. The primary legislation that permits initial nurse prescribing is the Medicinal Products: Prescription by Nurses Act 1992, but, although this Act was passed in 1992, the necessary secondary legislation, Medicinal Prescription by Nurses etc. (Commencement No. 1) Order 1994, did not come into effect until 3 October 1994.

Developing the initiative: the demonstration sites

On 21 November 1993, Baroness Cumberlege announced the introduction of demonstration sites for nurse prescribing, the purpose of the demonstration sites being to explore how the clinical, managerial and financial aspects of nurse prescribing could be managed effectively. GP fundholders and community units who could demonstrate commitment to nurse prescribing submitted a proforma to the DoH giving information about their unit and the fundholding practice. This was jointly signed by the practice, the community provider, the Family Health Service Authority and the region. The selection criteria for the demonstration sites included:

- evidence of an established GP fundholding practice
- a well-established primary health care team
- a contract for community services with a provider unit
- practice computing systems to enable linkage of patient and prescribing data
- the adequacy of management information systems
- a willingness to participate in data collection/evaluation prior to, during and after implementation
- the provision of representation on an implementation group and modification of the existing contract if necessary.

Eight sites were chosen, one in each of the health regions in England. The sites included inner city, rural and urban practices, some with large elderly populations and some with large numbers of children, especially the under 5s. Implementation in the eight demonstration sites was achieved by April 1994. The whole project was subject to an independent, fully researched evaluation which began in May 1994, to enable 'before and after' comparisons to be made. The University of Liverpool was commissioned to provide a qualitative evaluation of patient, nurse and doctor satisfaction with the scheme, and an analysis of the cost–benefit aspects of the scheme was undertaken by the University of York.

Two colleges of higher education (one in the north and one in the south of England) were invited to provide the taught component of the nurse prescribing course, and each submitted a detailed course document for validation by the English National

Board for Nursing, Midwifery and Health Visiting (ENB) in August 1994. After completing the *Nurse Prescribing: Open Learning Pack* (ENB 1994), nurses and health visitors in the prescribing sites attended one of these ENB-approved courses during September 1994 in readiness for commencing their nurse prescribing role in October 1994.

According to Jones and Gough (1997) 'with only eight sites involved, data from the project were not of sufficient statistical significance to extrapolate to the outcome of a national expansion of nurse prescribing.' Therefore in 1996, Bolton, one of the original pilot sites, was expanded to include 60 more practices, and a further 150 community nurses were trained as nurse prescribers. Two pilot sites were designated in Scotland in the same year. In 1997, following publication of the White Paper *Primary Care: Delivering the Future* (DoH 1996), a further seven pilot sites in NHS trusts were inaugurated in England, and the Bolton site was further extended to include Wigan. A press release in July 1997 announced that 'plans to extend nurse prescribing to Wales were unveiled as part of a package of primary health care measures announced by Welsh Health Minister Win Griffiths' (Scott 1997). These plans came to fruition when the first cohort of nurses started prescribing in January 2001. Training of approximately 1,500 nurses in Wales should be completed by March 2002 (Association for Nurse Prescribing 2001).

Preparation for nurse prescribing: education and training

In July 1991, the United Kingdom Central Council for Nursing, Midwifery and Health Visiting (UKCC) responded to the DoH's invitation to establish the standard, kind and content of educational preparation for nurse prescribing. It was recognised that the training should enable district nurses and health visitors to meet the learning outcomes set by the UKCC in order for them to prescribe safely and effectively from an appropriate knowledge base. According to the UKCC (1991, p. 1):

> in order to complete the preparation for nurse prescribing, individuals will need to ensure that they have sufficient knowledge of relevant pharmacology and therapeutics to enable them to undertake the programme. The *Nurses' Formulary* would provide the basis for identification of requirements.

The previous education and training of the course participants would also influence the type and length of programme required, in particular the amount of pre-course preparation necessary. The kind of programme envisaged by the UKCC would fall into two categories:

> A free standing module for district nurses and health visitors who are already qualified – and preparation which could be incorporated into the curriculum for district nursing and health visiting from a date agreed by the council.

> (UKCC 1991, p. 1)

A newsletter for institutions of higher education, issued by the ENB on July 1992, outlined the progress made with regard to the educational requirements for nurse prescribing. The following statement was incorporated:

> To ensure the availability of a suitable programme leading to the achieve-ment of competence and authority to prescribe, the ENB has been given responsibility and funding for developing and delivering:
>
> * an open learning pack
> * a video
> * guidance for the validation of programmes to be presented by institutions of higher education currently offering district nurse and health visitor courses.

> (ENB 1992)

A Steering Group with DoH and higher education represent-ation was set up in order to monitor and guide the preparation and development of the above. In order to ensure that the most effective strategies were employed, the Steering Group held a number of regional consultation days with district nurse and health visitor course leaders, formed a Working Group to plan and supervise the production of the open learning pack and appointed open learning consultants to advise the group and develop the materials. As stated in the ENB newsletter (1992), the Working Group represented:

> the major stakeholders in the process of preparing district nurses and health visitors for prescribing: practitioners, managers, lecturers, ENB directorate and the Department of Health.

The Group provided a wide range of professional expertise and also knowledge and experience of open learning.

The learning outcomes defined by the UKCC (1991, Section 5, p. 2) are:

- the ability to prescribe safely, effectively and cost-effectively from the Nurses' Formulary;
- an understanding of the potential side effects of, and reactions to, the items in the Nurses' Formulary;
- an understanding of the team and individual roles of doctors, dentists and pharmacists in relation to prescribing;
- an understanding of the requirements of the legislation relevant to the practice of nurse prescribing and
- an understanding of accountability and professional responsibility in relation to nurse prescribing.

One of the Working Group's main tasks was, based on the UKCC learning outcomes, to devise more specific outcomes for the *Open Learning Pack*. These were considered further in the light of information received from colleagues on the consultation days and from practitioner profiles taken from telephone interviews. It was decided that, in order to ensure integration of the *Open Learning Pack* and the taught component of the course, most topic areas should be included in both, the *Open Learning Pack* forming the bridge leading from the individual's current experience into the taught component. This would enable course participants to apply their existing knowledge and practice to nurse prescribing issues and to identify their own individual learning needs, which could be addressed in the taught part of the course.

The *Open Learning Pack* is divided into the following areas of study: getting to grips with nurse prescribing; accountability; prescribing safely and effectively; ethical issues; prescribing in a team context; administrative arrangements; and evaluating effectiveness. These topics were further developed in the taught course using a variety of teaching methods, including the ENB video, to trigger much discussion and debate. In addition, the taught course includes relevant pharmacology and therapeutics based on the NPF, together with other legal, financial and practical aspects of nurse prescribing.

The necessary training for nurse prescribing was outlined in the UKCC's response to an invitation from the DoH in July 1991. At that time, a two-day taught course component was recommended, but, following evaluations from the initial courses held in September 1994, the format of this part of the course was changed to three days, followed by an examination a week later. At present, nurses can only qualify by attending an ENB-approved course.

The UKCC (1991, p. 1) stated that:

> a variety of assessment strategies should be employed to test knowledge and synthesis and the application of theory to practice. Assessment should focus upon the principles of nurse prescribing, and the professional accountability and responsibility of the nurse undertaking the role.

Several assessment strategies were considered, including written examination, self-assessment, case study analysis, peer assessment, keeping a reflective journal and a defined period of supervised practice. However, as a matter of expediency, partly due to the tight timescale and the need to identify quickly whether course members were competent to prescribe in practice, the written examination was chosen. Most educationalists, given the essentially practical nature of nurse prescribing, would have preferred a combination of the other options, but the written examination, which is divided into two parts, proved to be a satisfactory method of assessment, for the following reasons. First, the short answer questions, some of which are multiple choice, are a useful way of ensuring a wide coverage of the curriculum and testing the principles of nurse prescribing. Second, the context-dependent questions based on case study analysis test knowledge of the nurse's role in prescribing situations and the understanding and application of identifying an appropriate rationale for decision-making in respect of nurse prescribing.

Assessment strategies are changing as the nurse prescribing initiative continues to be developed and is now an integral part of district nurse and health visitor education. With legislation now changed to include other branches of nursing, the course content, length of training and assessment have been reviewed in order to ensure that all nurses are prepared for their nurse prescribing role in the most appropriate manner. Now that there is a nucleus of experienced nurse prescribers across the country, it is easier to adopt a method of assessment which more accurately reflects practice, as there are nurses and health visitors acting as mentors/supervisors for those undertaking training. Indeed, nurse prescribing training is

subject to ongoing evaluation and review and as stated in paragraph
3.3 of *Nurse Prescribing Guidance*:

> In an effort to reduce infrastructure costs whilst maintaining the quality of
> training, further training models will be developed during the pilot trials and
> evaluated.
>
> (NHS Executive HQ, April 1997)

The ongoing monitoring and evaluation of the examination
procedure has enabled the strengths and weaknesses of the system
to be identified and minor modifications to be made. This knowledge will also help to ensure that an informed choice is made as
the assessment strategy is changed or modified.

Current examples of good practice now emerging from the
recent developments in nurse prescribing education include a
more integrated approach to assessment throughout the nurse
prescribing module; the use of work books as part of the examination procedure; presentation of appropriate assignments and case
studies which reflect integration of theory and practice. Many
courses for qualified district nurses and health visitors now incorporate a pre-course study day and more formalised tutorials while
students are studying the ENB *Open Learning Pack*. For those
nurses undertaking nurse prescribing training as an integral part of
their specialist practitioner programmes for district nursing and
health visiting, most courses have incorporated a period of supervised practice.

Nurse prescribing and primary health care

> Primary health care services are the first point of contact for most patients
> and their families, and are the most frequently used within the National
> Health Service. The skills, expertise, and knowledge base of all those who
> work in primary care have developed to meet challenges created by an
> increasingly more informed public, advances in technology, and better
> service outcomes.
>
> (Poulton 1997, p. 1)

The role of nurses and health visitors in primary health care has
developed to meet the changing health care needs of the population, and community nurses currently have a vital role to play in

a primary care-led NHS. Nurse prescribing has an important contribution to make in improving the service to patients and clients within the primary health care context. In fact, the potential advantages and benefits of nurse prescribing were clearly identified in the Crown Report (DoH 1989) and included improvement in patient care as nurses would be able to manage a patient's condition more effectively; a better use of patients' and nurses' time, thus enabling patients to receive treatment with the minimum of delay; and a clarification of professional responsibilities, which would strengthen professional partnership within the primary health care team.

The nurse, midwife or health visitor responsible for the programme of care for the patient or client is uniquely placed to make an accurate assessment of his or her needs based on a critical professional appraisal. For those nurses and health visitors who are trained as nurse prescribers, prescribing issues are an integral part of that assessment, and they utilise their clinical and professional judgement to decide when it is necessary to prescribe and which products from the NPF are the most appropriate to meet the needs identified. Community profiling and workload analysis will also enable nurses and health visitors to identify those patient/client groups and individuals most likely to require nurse-initiated prescriptions. Nurse prescribing will also impinge on the nurse's teaching and health promotion role. For example, patients experiencing problems with constipation may require advice about diet, fluid intake and variation in bowel habits, which will still be a first-line strategy in most cases; now, however, following a full clinical assessment, the nurse will be able to prescribe an appropriate laxative if this is necessary. The nurse is also in an ideal position to advise the patient on the action of the medication prescribed and to plan appropriate follow-up and evaluation of the situation for the care plan.

Have the potential benefits been realised in practice? It would appear so as, according to Luker et al. (1997a, p. 51):

> the advantages patients identified coincided with the anticipated benefits, while the disadvantages that had been anticipated before the study were not confirmed.

From the results of the study undertaken, it would appear that patients did receive treatment more promptly, and this was of great benefit to themselves and their carers. Luker et al. (1997a, p. 54) also state that:

> although it was anticipated that district nurses' patients would be the main beneficiaries of nurse prescribing, health visitor clients, in particular, were more likely to mention the increased convenience, practice nurses' patients, while benefiting overall, noted fewer changes.

These opinions reflected the relative ease or difficulty that each of these groups of patients had in obtaining a prescription before nurse prescribing. The reaction from patients and clients was extremely positive, and in some instances the nurse was cited as being the preferred prescriber. Patients quickly familiarised themselves with the nurses' remit, and there did not appear to be any undue confusion surrounding the nurses' and doctors' role in prescribing. According to Luker et al. (1997a, p. 54):

> patients were conscious of the fact that in the past the nurse had made the decision but the prescription had to be obtained from the GP. For these nurses this anomaly has now been rectified.

According to the Executive Summary of the *Evaluation of Nurse Prescribing. Final Report* (Luker et al. 1997b, pp. 12–13):

> There has been little reported change in professional relationships, between primary health care team members, with the notable exception of the pharmacist. District nurses reported a closer relationship with the pharmacist, HVs and PNs, who previously had very little, if any, contact now do have contact; this they have reported as being a positive aspect of nurse prescribing.

Also cited in this document is the fact that many professionals included in the evaluation indicated many advantages of nurse prescribing for patients and for the primary health care team. Time-saving was frequently mentioned; over half the GPs had noticed that nurse prescribing was saving them time and that they were signing fewer nurse-generated prescriptions, but in most cases this was not quantifiable. Luker et al. (1997b) also intimated that most nurses and health visitors participating in the demonstration sites had a positive reaction to nurse prescribing. The main benefits appear to be increased job satisfaction, time-saving and improved patient or client care, while the main frustration is the limited nature of the *Nurses' Formulary*, some nurses wanting to see additional items added to the list.

According to the *Open Learning Pack* (ENB 1994), teamwork is an essential part of nurse prescribing, and even those nurses working independently will have to report back to their nurse manager and have the opportunity to discuss their workload with other nurses and health visitors. For some practice nurses, this may not be quite so easy, and therefore the importance of the advantages of an integrated primary health care team, whose members have common goals and understand and respect each other's role and function within the team, cannot be overemphasised. Communication and teamwork are essential for effective nurse prescribing, one way of ensuring clear communication being to use well-defined local policies and/or protocols. In the interests of good patient or client care, it is also important to maintain good relationships with those nurses in the team who are unable to prescribe and keep them informed of any developments in the nurse prescribing initiative. In fact the summary of conclusions in the final report of the *Review of Prescribing, Supply and Administration of Medicines* (DoH 1999) states that their consultation:

> revealed considerable support for an extension of the groups of professionals who may prescribe, which would be expected to improve multidisciplinary team-work and make fullest use of professional skills

and also that:

> the extension of prescribing to new professional groups, subject to safeguards which would be established by the professional regulatory bodies, would yield benefits to patient care, improved patient convenience and better team-working between professionals.
>
> (p. 71)

Nurse prescribing: a changing role?

The future of nurse prescribing is a continuing and developmental process. A national roll-out of community nurse prescribing was announced in April 1998; however when there was prior indication of this, Bradley (1997) wrote:

The government intention, declared in recent white papers on primary care, is to roll out the nurse prescribing scheme to cover the whole country. All this would appear to imply that nurse prescribing has now arrived and is about to transform life for nurses, GPs and their patients. Well, don't you believe it. Unless the constraints currently operating on nurse prescribing are radically altered, the ability of nurses to prescribe will only ever have a very limited impact. The reasons for this are that nurse prescribing is confined to a restricted group of nurses (with district nursing or health visitor qualifications who have undergone further specific training) and to a fairly narrow formulary of drugs and appliances, most of which are available without prescription anyway. The result of these restrictions is that the majority of nurses who would like the power to prescribe *i.e.* practice nurses without the necessary qualifications, cannot do so. Furthermore, many of the items nurses would like to be able to prescribe, particularly those that enhance their role in chronic disease management, for example in asthma and diabetes, are precluded.

(p. 13)

However, although there are advocates for extending the NPF, there are also those who have expressed concern about nurses' knowledge of items already included in the *Formulary*. Some of these points are also borne out by Luker et al. (1997b) who state that since the publication of the first Crown Report (DoH 1989), considerable changes have taken place in the role of nurses working in the community. This particularly applies to practice nurses whose role is very diverse and has developed considerably since the implementation of the GP contract (DoH and Welsh Office 1990). Atkin et al. (1993) in a national consensus of practice nurses, identified that about 96% of practice nurses were involved in the provision of immunisations, almost 30% in family planning, 55% in diabetes management and 52% in asthma management. The extension of the practice nurse's role has led to much discussion as to whether the *Nurses' Formulary* is too restrictive especially in relation to chronic disease management, for example care of the asthmatic patient.

Luker et al. (1997c) point out that although the role of the practice nurse has expanded there is a diversity of expertise among this group and considerable variation in the qualifications they possess. Variations in preparation for practice, of which practice nursing is an example, will need to be considered when planning the future education of nurse prescribers. These concerns reinforce the point that it is essential for all nurses to be properly and appropriately trained before undertaking additional professional responsibilities. Have recent developments suggested changes which may allay some of these fears?

The long-awaited *Final Report* (DoH 1999) of a Working Group chaired by Dr June Crown which was set up by the government to review prescribing, supply and administration of medicines (known as Crown II) was published in March 1999. In the accompanying letter to the Rt Hon Frank Dobson MP, then Secretary of State for Health, the following paragraphs were included:

> The Review Team have considered carefully the extensive evidence that was submitted during the period of consultation. It is inevitable that we could not produce recommendations which would meet all the aspirations expressed to us, while at the same time meeting your requirements for a robust framework for an extension which safeguards patient safety.
>
> The team believes, however, that its proposals, if implemented, will provide a secure means of increasing the range of health professionals who are authorised to prescribe. This will improve services to patients, make better use of the skills of professional staff and thus make a significant contribution to the modernisation of the health service.

This detailed report which includes many conclusions and recommendations, was presented to the professions for comment in March 1999 and a six-month consultation period was granted. Some of the conclusions and recommendations that have a particular relevance to nurse education and practice are highlighted as follows. One of the conclusions reached indicates that:

> professional practice is changing in response to changing patterns of clinical care, professional education and patient expectations. These trends have not been fully reflected in the arrangements for the prescribing, supply and administration of medicines.
>
> (DoH 1999, p. 71)

Increasingly, within the general practice setting, practice nurses who have undergone further specific training, for example a Diploma in Asthma Care, may be running nurse-led clinics and advising patients of the most appropriate medication to control and improve their medical condition but they are unable to prescribe this medication and currently have to generate a prescription from the GP. This is seen by some nurses to be very frustrating and potentially time wasting and, as Luker et al. (1997c) argue, practice nurses already influence the prescribing behaviour of GPs

in the areas of asthma and diabetes and the nurse's ability and practice have 'outstripped' the parameters of the NPF.

The Crown II Report (DoH 1999) which covers a much wider
remit than community nurses with a district nurse or health visitor
qualification, outlines in some detail the importance of appropriate professional training for all new prescribers. The recommendations have profound implications for professional training
especially as other professions such as pharmacists, optometrists
and podiatrists could be granted prescribing powers if the report
is implemented. The recommendations also encompass other
nursing groups, including those in specialist therapeutic areas
such as asthma. One could argue that community nurses have had
a head-start as far as training and prescribing practice are
concerned, especially as some of the guidance for training in the
Crown II Report replicates what is currently happening in the
community nurse education field, for example:

> training programmes for prescribing would need to be set up in the first
> instance for those health professionals who have already obtained the
> necessary specialist clinical qualification.

(p. 66)

However the recommendation that:

> all training should include a period of supervised practice, and professional
> and regulatory bodies should take firm action against supervisors who fail to
> discharge their responsibilities

(p. 66)

may have implications for the assessment and curriculum design of
future community nurse education nurse prescribing modules.
This model is a familiar one that has been utilised for many years
in health visitor and district nurse education but has not yet been
incorporated into all of the current nurse prescribing programmes.

Current situation

In spite of its critics nurse prescribing is a major step forward for
nurses and one which has, in the main, been met with a very positive and enthusiastic response, having been seen to have strength-

ened teamwork in primary care in some instances. Patients appear to have welcomed the initiative and GPs and pharmacists have been very supportive. According to Brooks et al. (2001) patients view nurse prescribing as a practical and responsive method of service delivery although some concern was expressed regarding the limitations of the *Nurse Prescribers' Formulary*.

Community nurses have pioneered the nurse prescribing initiative and for many this is now an integral and important part of their clinical care. The uniqueness of their role has been emphasised in that they are well versed with the needs of each patient/client and of the services and resources available to help meet those needs. This knowledge and experience enable them to provide a service tailored to individual needs and circumstances.

Nurse prescribing initiatives are moving on apace and it would appear that rolling out the nurse prescribing initiative to all those nurses with a health visitor or district nurse qualification and currently practising in their relevant fields is only the beginning. However, by April 2001 it was estimated that there were 23,000 qualified nurse prescribers.

In 1997, Jones and Gough stated:

> For nurse prescribing to find full expression appropriate to the demands of today's health services and the expanding nature of nursing practice, the existing legislation needs urgent revision.
>
> (p. 42)

They also advocated the lifting of restrictions on the type of nurse able to prescribe and the expansion of the *Nurses' Formulary*. The government announced on 13 March 2000, that it had accepted and would take forward the main recommendations of the *Review of Prescribing, Supply and Administration of Medicines*. This included extending the scope of nurse prescribing, which does not require primary legislation, and also extending prescribing rights to other health professionals when parliamentary time allows. The government consultation paper on extending independent nurse prescribing (DoH 2000) was welcomed by nurses as it outlines options for extending the *Nurse Prescribers' Formulary* and indicates a range of medical conditions which nurses could be trained to prescribe for. The consultation period ended on 10 January 2001 and on 5 May 2001 a press release from the DoH gave information that a further 10,000 nurses will undergo training to become prescribers.

Conclusion

Nurses and health visitors currently able to prescribe acknowledge that nurse prescribing is very much an integral part of their role and hope that this aspect of their work will continue to develop as it increases job satisfaction and is enabling them to provide a more comprehensive service. With the advent of further developments in nurse prescribing, both in terms of the nurses who may prescribe and the expanded *Nurse Formulary*, this valued component of nursing should be further enhanced.

References

Association for Nurse Prescribing (2001) *Nurse Prescribing Handbook.* Emap Healthcare, London.

Atkin, K., Lunt, N., Park, G. and Hirst, M. (1993) *Nurse Count: A National Census of Practice Nurses.* Social Policy Research Unit, York.

Blatt, B. (1997) Nurse prescribing: Are you ready? *Practice Nursing,* 8(12): 11–13.

Bradley, C. (1997) Nurse prescribing – unlikely to transform our lives. *Prescriber,* 5 May 1997: 13.

Brooks, N., Otway, C., Rashid, S., Kilty, L. and Maggs, C. (2001) Nurse prescribing: what do patients think? *Nursing Standard,* 15(17): 33–8.

DHSS (1986) *Neighbourhood Nursing – A Focus for Care* (Cumberlege Report). HMSO, London.

DoH (1989) *Report of the Advisory Group on Nurse Prescribing* (Crown Report). DoH, London.

DoH (1996) *Primary Care: Delivering the Future.* HMSO, London.

DoH (1999) *Review of Prescribing, Supply and Administration of Medicines. Final Report* (Crown II Report). DoH, London.

DoH (2000) *Consultation on Proposals to Extend Nurse Prescribing.* DoH, London.

DoH and Welsh Office (1990) *Terms and Conditions for Doctors in General Practice.* The NHS (General Medical and Pharmaceutical Services) Regulations 1974 Schedules 1–3 as amended. HMSO, London.

ENB (1992) *Nurse Prescribing: Newsletter for Institutions of Higher Education.* ENB, London.

ENB (1994) *Nurse Prescribing: Open Learning Pack.* ENB, London.

Jones, M. and Gough, P. (1997) Nurse prescribing – why has it taken so long? *Nursing Standard*, 11(20).
Luker, K.A., Austin, L., Hogg. C., Ferguson, B. and Smith, K. (1997a) Patients' views of nurse prescribing. *Nursing Times*, 93(17): 51–4.
Luker, K.A., Austin, L., Hogg. C. et al. (1997b) Evaluation of Nurse Prescribing. Final Report: Executive Summary. Unpublished report.
Luker, K.A., Austin, L., Willock, J., Ferguson, B. and Smith, K. (1997c) Nurses' and GPs' views of the *Nurse Prescribers' Formulary*. *Nursing Standard*, 11(22): 33–8.
NHS Executive HQ (1997) *Nurse Prescribing Guidance April 1997*. NHS Executive HQ, Leeds.
Poulton, B. (1997) *Practice Nursing: A Changing Role to Meet Changing Need*. DoH, London.
Scott, G. (1997) Welsh nurses elated as prescribing arrives. *Nursing Standard*, 11(44).
UKCC (1991) *The Council's Response to the Department of Health's Invitation to Establish the Standard, Kind and Content of Educational Preparation for Nurse Prescribing*. July 30th 1991. UKCC, London.

2

Nurse prescribing: ethical principles and accountability

Eileen Groves

Introduction

Nursing is in essence a dynamic process and current practice has advanced nursing far beyond its traditional boundaries (Fletcher et al. 1995). Changes in nurse education and social and political influences have all shaped, and will continue to shape, the face of nursing. For example, many nurses now take on board tasks traditionally undertaken by doctors, which include, in some situations, the supply and administration of medicines within set protocols. Sometimes change has been gradual and insidious, at others sudden and dramatic, or as a result of legislation such as the Medicinal Products: Prescription by Nurses Act 1992, which opened the door for nurse prescribing.

As the role of the nurse continues to develop and expand so do the scope and range of professional responsibilities and thus, accordingly, accountability. Once new skills and tasks become incorporated into the individual nurse's role, accountability becomes an integral part of it. A dictionary definition of accountability would tell us that it is to be responsible, liable and explicable for our actions (*Little Oxford Dictionary* 1969).

This chapter seeks to explore the nature of professional accountability and its application to nurse prescribing. Accountability within the legal framework will be explored in Chapter 3.

Professional accountability

Historical perspectives

> In my estimation obedience is the first law and very cornerstone of good nursing. And here is the stumbling block for the beginner. No matter how

gifted she may be she will never become a reliable nurse unless she can obey without question. The first and most helpful criticism I received from a doctor was when he told me that I was supposed to be simply an intelligent machine for the purposes of carrying out his orders.

(Dock 1917)

It comes as no surprise to note the date of this much-published quote: such sentiments today would spark widespread reaction and would do little to foster interprofessional relationships between the medical and nursing professions. Yet it has to be remembered that such comment simply reflected the social and gender traditions and ideologies of the era. The nurse in this context was seen as a 'handmaiden' and, as Brown et al. (1992) suggest, 'diligent, hardworking, trustworthy and loyal, conscientious in her duties and using her special nurturing skills to provide comfort to patients so that the real work of medicine might not be impeded' (p. 75). Within such an environment, nurses were accountable to the person making decisions regarding patient care, be it the medical practitioner or the management organisation.

Nursing has clearly advanced considerably since then, establishing itself as a profession in its own right with the introduction of the nursing process and nursing models in the 1980s, giving nursing its own unique body of knowledge; and documents from the UKCC, for example the *Code of Professional Conduct* (1992a) and the *Scope of Professional Practice* (1992b), stressing the individual accountability of the nurse. As we are frequently reminded, 'acting on doctor's orders' is no defence in law. Nurses are now expected to act as advocates for patients and clients, and as such may sometimes need to challenge the decisions of medical colleagues or management.

Koehn (1994) suggests that the use of the title 'professional' normally applies to those whose work is:

- licensed by the state
- controlled by an organisation which sets standards and ideals
- such that its members have knowledge and skills not normally possessed or understood by the general public
- such that they have autonomy over their work
- of a nature that requires them to have responsibilities and duties to those who need assistance, responsibilities which are not incumbent on others.

It might be argued, then, that it is only in recent years, with the concept of individual accountability, that nurses have truly had the level of autonomy to take on board the title 'professional'.

Contemporary perspectives

The advent of nurse prescribing further enhances the notions of autonomy and professional status. The UKCC guidelines currently regulate nursing practice in this country by using the *Code of Professional Conduct* (1992a), as a standard against which criteria for good nursing practice may be set and any allegations of misconduct measured. As a body, the UKCC is statutorily obliged to regulate the standard and practice of its members:

> A professional code represents a statement of the role morality of the members of the profession, and in this way professional standards are distinguished from standards imposed by external bodies such as government (although their norms sometimes overlap and agree).
>
> (Beauchamp and Childress 1994, p. 7)

The response to changing health care needs and changing health care provision has greatly increased the scope of practice for the nurse and helped further to develop the professionalisation of nursing and all that such status brings with it, not least individual accountability. Nurse prescribing is one such example of the increase in the scope of practice afforded to suitably qualified nurses, which initially included qualified district nurses, health visitors and practice nurses with a district nurse or health visitor qualification. Extending prescribing to other groups of nurses is currently underway. Future extensions are also likely by allowing certain nurses to become supplementary prescribers, for example those qualified to work as asthma or diabetes nurses. As nursing practice continues to change, so details of professional accountability may change over time although the underlying notion of accountability will remain the same. Accountability is a dynamic process to which nurses will have to adapt and link their individual roles and functions to a set code of professional practice, which will also change over time. As in all other areas of nursing practice, accountability in prescribing is primarily to the patient/client and extends to the employing body, colleagues, the UKCC and ultimately the law.

It is not the intention of the author to examine every possible accountability issue that may arise for the nurse prescriber, as individual practice will bring its own range of issues. Neither will it be possible to give definitive answers to the many questions that may be raised – in fact, it is probable that there will be more questions raised than answers offered. It is simply the intention to raise awareness of the extent of accountability in nurse prescribing.

Accountability within the health care professions has assumed a high profile within the past decade as the growth in litigation within health care generally has seen a dramatic rise, health care professionals being held accountable for careless actions or omissions. The notion of accountability is implicit within all elements of the *Code of Professional Conduct* (UKCC 1992a) and arises directly out of responsibility. To be accountable, there has to be some authority to act and a basis of knowledge and competency that can be explained and defended:

> Codes of conduct only make sense in the light of accountability. They are only worth something if they can be tested, that is if professionals can be held accountable for decisions and their behaviour.
>
> (ENB 1994)

Tadd (1994) suggests that the concept of professional accountability disregards the fact that not all practitioners are fully autonomous or hold sufficient power in all aspects of their work to be held to account. However, in the area of nurse prescribing, all nurses eligible to prescribe will have power and authority to make prescribing decisions, and as such will be accountable both legally and professionally (ENB 1994).

Nurses who prescribe will be accountable for all aspects of the prescribing process, from the decision to prescribe, to ensuring that the prescription is applied or administered as directed either by the nurse or by the relatives or carers if they are given the medication to administer.

> The nurse who takes the initial decision and writes the prescription is responsible in law for ensuring that the prescription is used in accordance with the instructions.
>
> (ENB 1994, Section 2, p. 2)

This accountability will also include decisions taken in recommending over-the-counter prescriptions and being responsible for the decision not to prescribe.

Once dispensed, rules governing the safety, storage and administration of drugs, as set out in the *Guidelines for the Administration of Medicines* (UKCC 2000) and *Standards for Records and Record Keeping* (UKCC 1998), will apply. Accountability in nursing is clearly not new, and extends to actions, omissions, spheres of influence, delegation or acquiescence in respect of the public, employers and, of course, oneself. Once prescribing has been encompassed into the nurse's role and a prescribing situation presents itself, accountability extends not only to treatment prescribed (action) but also treatment omitted.

> Ensure that no action or omission on your part, or within your sphere of responsibility, is detrimental to the interests, condition or safety of patients and clients.
>
> (UKCC 1992a, ol. 2)

The *Scope of Professional Practice* (UKCC 1992b) builds on the *Code of Professional Conduct* (UKCC 1992a) and this concept of individual accountability.

As nursing practice continued to develop in the 1980s, and nurses began to undertake 'extended' duties as a matter of course, it was no longer practicable to continue with the system of collecting certificates of competence for 'extended practice'. The *Scope of Professional Practice* was designed to enable nurses to provide continuity of care and holistic care to patients and clients for whom they are responsible. Nurses no longer accumulate a wide range of certificates stating their competence to practise, rather they are asked to make individual decisions regarding their competence to carry out such procedures and be individually accountable for their practice. While it might be seen to be in patients' interests to have fewer people involved in their care, and it could also be viewed as being in the interests of the personal and professional development of the individual nurse, it does however place full responsibility on the nurses to determine the skills required for particular procedures and to ensure that they are appropriately qualified to carry them out. It is therefore incumbent on the individual nurse to ensure that his or her practice is not only safe, but also up to date and research based:

Acknowledge any limitations in your knowledge and competence and decline any duties or responsibilities unless able to perform them in a safe and skilled manner.

(UKCC 1992a, cl. 4)

Accountability is an integral part of professional practice. As the scope of professional practice continues to widen, nurses are required to make judgements on a wide range of health care issues. Given the increasing emphasis on individual accountability in nursing and the need to be able to explain and be liable for right or wrong actions, it is perhaps pertinent to explore further this concept of accountability from ethical perspectives, with some examples from nurse prescribing practice.

Ethical theory and principles

In order to fully appreciate the ethical perspective it is perhaps useful to offer a brief overview of ethical theory and principles as applied to health care. The words 'ethics', from the Greek, and 'morals', from the Latin, will be used interchangeably; both in definition originally meant much the same. Morals could be said to be the beliefs and values used to determine the rights and wrongs of human behaviour in general terms (Thompson et al. 1994). Health care ethics has its roots in moral philosophy and is concerned with the character and conduct of individuals in the pursuance of good practice that meets these moral values and beliefs. Thompson et al. (1994) state that both are concerned with 'the general area of rights and wrongs, in theory and practice, of human behaviour' (p. 3).

It is not within the scope of this chapter to develop ethics as a topic in great detail, and the author accepts that a somewhat pragmatic approach has been taken in order to illustrate the place of ethics within the nurse prescribing role.

Background

Rumbold (1999) suggests that the study of ethics is concerned with examining words such as 'right', 'wrong', 'good', 'bad', 'ought' and 'duty'. It is concerned with the way in which people either individually or collectively make decisions about what actions are right or wrong and what people ought or ought not be able to do to one another. The study of ethics seeks to provide answers to such questions and guide the way in which people deal with ethical dilemmas.

As health care professionals we bring to our work our own beliefs, attitudes and values, all of which, in a continually evolving social structure and culture, may well be different from those of the patients and clients with whom we deal professionally. This is not surprising as each of us has our in-built value system based on family values and norms, educational, cultural and social influences and the peer group influences we are exposed to socially and professionally in our lives.

It therefore follows that patient/client views on the rights and wrongs of prescribed treatment or health education and advice may well differ from the professionals. Consider the implications of this for the prescriber in terms of acceptability of treatment, concordance with treatment or of advice given on diet or hygiene, and how this relates to accountability.

Throughout their lives, people may at some time or other be held accountable for their actions, either legally, morally or simply in a neutral way, to others (Fletcher et al. 1995). For example, if we break the law we will be held accountable to the judicial system for our actions; and if we upset or offend someone by our action or inaction, we may be morally accountable for the harm we have caused. Or it may simply be that, in our ordinary, everyday lives, we are accountable to others in a more neutral way for the choices we make about what we do, how we spend our time or how we use our money. In each situation, Fletcher et al. (1995) suggest that it may be possible to give reasons for our actions, which will range from very good to none at all.

In health care, ethics and law go hand in hand as the law simply reflects society's views on acceptable ethical standards of practice from health care professionals. A nurse may therefore be held to account both legally and morally for the actions that he or she carries out.

Ethical issues, along with legal issues, in health care have assumed a high profile in recent years, particularly in emotive areas such as abortion, in vitro fertilisation and euthanasia, but it is often in ordinary, everyday work situations that nurses face difficult decisions that may have an ethical dimension.

Ethics then, is concerned with the rights and wrongs of human behaviour, and in health care ethics it is about right and wrong actions, and about the responsibilities, obligations and duties we have to patients and clients to ensure that all our actions are right actions.

Health care professionals have the unique privilege of intervening in someone's life at a time when they are most vulnerable, that is, they are ill or in need of help and support in a health care matter. It is important therefore that every effort is made to ensure that any intervention, practical or advisory, stands up to the highest moral scrutiny.

Ethical problems arise when there are at least two possible courses of action that can be taken, each of which might bring about the same, or indeed a different, result.

Ethical dilemmas occur when we are faced with a situation that appears irresolvable, or if the solution offers alternatives that we find difficult because they may compromise or conflict with our existing moral values of what we feel is a good or right course of action in a particular set of circumstances. Health care professionals are concerned with ensuring that the action they take is right and can be justified against all other possible options, in other words applying what Thompson et al. (1994) call 'reasoned judgement'. This requires:

> Skills in assessment of moral situations, informed deliberation on practical and ethical options, ability to act decisively and competently, and critical evaluation of outcomes in terms of cost and benefit.
>
> (Thompson et al., p. x)

Application to prescribing issues

The ethical principles of autonomy and respect for autonomy, beneficence (to do good), non-maleficence (to do no harm) and justice, underpin nurses' *Code of Professional Conduct* (UKCC 1992a). Such principles, Beauchamp and Childress (1994) maintain, should be prima facie, (without question), and easily understood by all health care workers as it would be expected that anyone working within the field of health care would aspire to such concepts. They also go on to suggest, however, that codes of professional conduct invariably stress rules of dos and don'ts in respect of the above, particularly 'above all do no harm', rather than the implications of wider principles and rules concerned with veracity, respect for autonomy and justice. For example an individual's autonomy can be severely compromised if they are not given sufficient information regarding proposed treatment to make an informed choice. This includes information not only about the benefits, but possible side-effects, contraindications, and length of time it might take for improvement to be noticed.

Autonomy may be defined as self-rule or self-governance, and Harris (1985) likens it to 'living one's own life according to one's lights', as they are perceived at any one particular time. Clearly there are social, cultural and legal limits to complete autonomy otherwise any actions, good or bad, could be sanctioned in the name of autonomy. A general rule is that autonomy should be respected in so far as it does not interfere with the autonomy of another (Beauchamp and Childress 1994).

Clearly in times of ill health, disease or infirmity an individual's autonomy may well be compromised or diminished. If, as Beauchamp and Childress (1994) suggest, autonomy should be a prima facie principle, then health care activities should be directed towards respecting autonomy, enhancing an individual's potential to be maximally autonomous, and protecting those whose autonomy has been lost.

Traditionally in health care there has been a culture of paternalism whereby the overriding of autonomy has been justified on the basis of acting 'in the patient's best interests' and following obligations of 'duty to care' (Gillon 1985). That culture is now changing and people are being encouraged in all areas of their lives to make informed choices about the options available to them, and this includes health care options. This has implications for accountability and informed consent, an area that will be covered in the following chapter relating to the legal issues in nurse prescribing.

Beneficence and non-maleficence are often viewed alongside one another, as there is potential for tensions between the two. For example it could be argued that harm in health care treatments can sometimes be unavoidable: side-effects of drugs in chemotherapy; the discomfort of a compression bandage; necessary surgical intervention; but harm related to adverse interaction of medication or the development of iatrogenic disease as a result of poor prescribing should be avoidable with sound assessment skills and evidence-based practice.

Codes of Professional Practice and Conduct are particularly concerned with the responsibilities, duties and obligations of professionals within the nurse–patient/client working and caring relationship rather than with any rights of entitlement that the client may have. In recent years, however, we have seen various rights afforded to citizens, and in health care we have seen the introduction of *The Patient's Charter* (DoH 1992), which highlights those patients' rights that have to be addressed, alongside the professional responsibilities, obligations and duties of the nurse. Resource implications often make it difficult to reconcile the two.

Rights automatically imply that someone has a duty to provide for those rights to be fulfilled. Knowing a patient's rights of entitlement and being unable to fulfil those rights due to financial or organisational constraints creates stress, tension and ethical dilemmas for the practitioner in terms of the fair and just allocation of resources. It is worth remembering too that one of the most precious resources we have is that of our time. How we allocate this can create as many tensions as deciding on allocation of material resources. While nurse prescribing might in the long term be time and cost-effective, and certainly in the patient/client interest, taking on board the whole remit of the prescribing role from assessment to evaluation and reflection, can be a time intensive, albeit rewarding and valuable, exercise if it is to be undertaken safely and effectively. Ethical rules and principles are complex topics and demand further exploration and discussion outside the remit of this chapter.

Other ethical issues may arise as nurses strive to encompass wider role responsibilities to relatives and colleagues, employers and the public. Conflicts may arise for the nurse prescriber in the attitudes and possible resistance of colleagues and other health care professionals to their prescribing role, differences in case loads, the expectations of patients and clients, and the questioning of the resource implications in terms of time and finance. In such situations, nurses need to look at how best the patients' interests may be served:

Act always in such a manner as to promote and safeguard the interests and
well-being of patients and clients.

(UKCC 1992a, cl. 1)

Clearly, if the responsibilities within nurse prescribing are to range
from decisions of if and when to prescribe, to ensuring correct
administration, there may well be ethical dilemmas along the way.
The ENB (1994) *Nurse Prescribing: Open Learning Pack* highlights areas that may pose ethical problems or dilemmas for nurses
both from within the nurse–patient/client role and in the wider
responsibilities that the nurse prescribing role brings.

For example, is there a need to compromise on your choice of
prescribed treatment because of local protocol, primary care
group/trust formularies, cost or limited availability in the choice
of generic products? Is there patient pressure to prescribe? Will
the patient co-operate with an assessment or visit the GP if recommended? If recommending over-the-counter medication, what
are the choices available? What can the patient afford? Can the
patient afford to pay for medication rather than be given a
prescription, thereby possibly releasing monies for others less able
to pay? Are there pressures from drug companies and appliance
manufacturers to persuade you to prescribe or use their particular
products? For example, free trials of a special dressing may
produce good results for the patient, but if that dressing is not in
the NPF, or is too expensive to continue with once the free supply
is ended, what happens then? There are many occasions on which
we may be persuaded to try different brands of goods or products
in our daily lives, and we all know how convincing such sales talk
can be. It would clearly be impossible to read in depth all the
research papers regarding new products, but, if we are to apply
the maxim, 'Above all do no harm', nurses at least need to be
aware of any possible or potential side-effects or contraindications
of the products they prescribe. The principles of evidence-based
practice are apparent, even the simplest of dressings can cause
allergic reactions. Given all these possible scenarios, how does the
nurse choose the right courses of action when faced with ethical
problems or dilemmas?

Ethical theory: application to prescribing

Ethical theory would offer many possible ways of looking at the same problem. It would be impracticable here to enter into a great debate and discussion on the various ethical theories and ethical decision-making frameworks that abound. However, it is perhaps worth exploring two possible approaches commonly used within health care ethics to illustrate the way in which ethical dilemmas can be approached from differing perspectives to meet those underlying principles of autonomy and respect for autonomy, beneficence, non-maleficence and justice previously discussed.

First, there is the deontological (duty) approach, which suggests that ethical dilemmas are best resolved by taking a duty-based approach, following moral rules, to the problem. That is, looking at the problem in terms of what one's duty and obligations are to the patient or client and planning a course of action accordingly, irrespective of the consequences. Right actions and results taking this approach are therefore said to be those where one follows one's duty. One of the main proponents of this theory was Immanuel Kant, an 18th-century German philosopher.

The other approach that may be taken suggests that the right solution to an ethical dilemma will be found in taking actions that will lead to the maximisation of welfare and the greatest good for all concerned (utilitarianism). This is essentially a goal-based or consequentialist approach as one has to have some goal or end in mind in order to direct one's actions towards that which maximises welfare and brings about the greater good. Two of the best known proponents of this theory are Jeremy Bentham and John Stuart Mill, 19th-century English philosophers (Gillon 1985; Beauchamp and Childress 1994).

An example from nurse prescribing practice that highlights these two differing approaches might be that of a patient whom you have assessed, recognising that a particular brand of cream will be most effective for the speedy healing of his leg ulcer, thereby promoting his autonomy. However, you know that it is extremely expensive, you have a budget to maintain, and you have two other patients still to assess who might also benefit from this cream. Do you take a deontological approach and carry out your duties and responsibilities to the first patient? Or do you prescribe a cheaper cream that may take longer to heal the ulcer, but with a view of maximising welfare, that is, treating them all for the same cost as it would have been to treat the first person with the expensive product?

Or, perhaps worse still, you may be placed in a position of having to assess the relative needs of one patient over another, possibly being forced to make value judgements about need that may require the aggregation of one person's welfare over another's, perhaps using quality of life as a measurement tool (Gillon 1985). Does this place the nurse in situations where duties may have to be compromised in favour of the greater good approach? Gillon (1985) suggests that taking a greater good route could leave the individual in a perpetual state of jeopardy and questions whether such an approach might lead to the justification of ignoring the basic moral principles of right and good actions.

Such circumstances clearly highlight the way in which those ethical principles relating to autonomy, beneficence, non-maleficence and justice might affect prescribing decisions and the difficulties in deciding the approach to be taken.

Case studies

Consider the following case scenarios and examine them from a professional, a prescribing and an ethical perspective, applying the principles of respect for autonomy, beneficence, non-maleficence and justice.

Case Scenario 1

Andy and Jane are 17-year-old parents of ten-week-old Jamie. They live in a privately rented flat that is basic but appears clean and well cared for. Andy has part-time evening bar work and Jane hopes to resume part-time work as a shop assistant when Jamie is 3 months old. Jamie is brought by his mother to a busy clinic for a routine weight check. While he appears generally to be thriving, he has an extensive, 'angry' nappy rash, which is clearly causing him some distress. Jamie is primarily breastfed with occasional supplemental bottle feeds. Jane is anxious to be seen as a competent mother and is clearly upset by Jamie's condition.

Case Scenario 2

John Miller is a 45-year-old self-employed builder who has undergone surgery for repair of a right inguinal hernia three weeks ago. The wound was infected initially and the GP prescribed a course of antibiotics. John attends the health centre for a final check on his wound. The wound has now healed well and he is anxious to return to work as soon as possible. However, he is concerned that he is still experiencing some discomfort and occasional pain in his right side. He also complains of constipation and seeks your advice on suitable laxatives.

Case Scenario 3

Julie Brown is a thirty-year-old single parent with two children under school age. With the help and support of her mother, who lives nearby, and the children's father, who cares for them on alternate weekends, Julie is able to undertake part-time work at a local petrol station. Julie visits the well persons' clinic for routine cervical cytology. During the consultation she tells you she is experiencing recurrent headaches that are disturbing her sleep, and has an itchy rash on her hands and arms. Julie asks if you can prescribe for both of these problems.

The professional issues will no doubt be clearly apparent. Try also to tease out the potential prescribing issues, justify your decision and address how you might promote, maintain and respect the autonomy of the individuals concerned, balance the tensions between beneficence and non-maleficence and consider any elements of justice and fairness that might influence your decision.

The whole area of the study of ethics is exciting and demands that we closely examine our decision-making processes in often complex ethical dilemmas if we are to ensure that the actions we take are right actions for all concerned. Further study of the ethics of health care is recommended.

Conclusion

As the role of the nurse continues to develop and increase with advances in medical science and technology and wider issues, such as the current political climate that calls for a reduction in junior doctors' hours so placing more responsibility on the nurse, nurses must continue to be guided by the *Code of Professional Conduct* (UKCC 1992a) and the *Scope of Professional Practice* (UKCC 1992b). Both these documents stress the importance of maintaining professional knowledge and competence, and emphasise the personal responsibility and accountability for practice. Any nurse who undertakes a task for which he or she is not trained or competent may be held accountable to his or her professional body; if the patient suffers harm, the nurse may be liable for negligence and held to account by the law, the profession or both. It is thus vital that all nurses engaging in nurse prescribing do not simply complete the necessary course but are able to take on board all the ongoing responsibilities that go with their new role.

References

Beauchamp, T.L. and Childress, J.F. (1994) *Principles of Biomedical Ethics*, 4th edn. Oxford University Press, Oxford.

Brown, J.M., Kitson, A.L. and McKnight T.J. (1992) *Challenges in Caring*. Chapman & Hall, London.

Dock, S. (1917) The relation of the nurse to the doctor and the doctor to the nurse. *American Journal of Nursing*, 17: 394.

DoH (1992) *The Patient's Charter*. HMSO, London.

DoH (2000) *Consultation on Proposals to Extend Nurse Prescribing*. http://www.doh.gov.uk/nurseprescribing/index.htm.

ENB (1994) *Nurse Prescribing: Open Learning Pack*. ENB, London.

Fletcher, N., Holt, J., Brazier M. and Harris, J. (1995) *Ethics Law and Nursing*. Manchester University Press, Manchester.

Gillon R. (1985) *Philosophical Medical Ethics*. Wiley, Chichester.

Harris J. (1985) *The Value of Life, An Introduction to Medical Ethics*. Routledge, London.

Koehn, D. (1994) *The Groundwork of Professional Ethics*. Routledge, London.

Little Oxford Dictionary of Current English (4th edn) (1969) Clarendon Press, Oxford.

Rumbold, G. (1999) Ethics in Nursing Practice (3rd edn). Baillière Tindall, London.

Tadd, V. (1994) Professional codes: an exercise in tokenism. *Nursing Ethics*, **1**(1): 15–23.

Thompson, I.E., Melia, K.M. and Boyd, K.M. (1994) *Nursing Ethics.* Churchill Livingstone, Edinburgh.

UKCC (1992a) *Code of Professional Conduct.* UKCC, London.

UKCC (1992b) *Scope of Professional Practice.* UKCC, London.

UKCC (1998) *Standards for Records and Record Keeping.* UKCC, London.

UKCC (2000) *Guidelines for the Administration of Medicines.* UKCC, London.

3

Nurse prescribing: accountability and legal issues

Steven Preece

Nurse prescribing: summary of the present legal position

Although it is more than 30 years old and reflects practice at that time, the Medicines Act of 1968 remains effective. Perhaps more than any other single piece of legislation the Medicines Act constrains changes in practice for health professionals. The Act restricts the prescribing of prescription-only medicines to, 'appropriate practitioners', defined in the Act as registered medical practitioners, registered dental practitioners and registered veterinary practitioners. The Medicinal Products: Prescription by Nurses Act 1992, and subsequent legislation under that Act, permits certain nurses to prescribe a limited range of drugs and medicinal products within the *Nurse Prescribers' Formulary*. The criteria for a nurse to be allowed to prescribe are that he or she is a first-level nurse with a district nurse or health visitor qualification. The nurse must be working within a primary health care setting as a health visitor, district nurse or practice nurse and be authorised to prescribe by his or her employer. In addition, all nurse prescribers must have successfully completed the nurse prescriber course and be registered as a nurse prescriber by the UKCC (NHS Executive 1998a).

In May 2001 the Department of Health announced further extensions to prescribing rights for nurses. In July 2001 the Medicines Control Agency published a consultation document recommending extensions to prescribing by 'independent' nurse prescribers. First-level nurses, who after training are recognised as independent nurse prescribers, will have scope to prescribe all general sales list and pharmacy medicines prescribable by doctors under the NHS, except for certain drugs which are subject to control under the Misuse of Drugs legislation. They will also be able to prescribe from a list of prescription-only medicines (POMs) relating to the four treatment areas of minor ailments, minor injuries, health promotion and palliative care (see Appendix 2 for proposed list). Consultation on 'supplementary' prescribing, by nurses is expected later in 2001. As supplementary prescribers, that is to say prescribing for patients who have previously been clinically assessed by a doctor, appropriately trained and experienced nurses will have scope to prescribe for more complex conditions and chronic disease. In all circumstances nurse prescribers are bound by the legal duty on all professionals to act only within their expertise and even where regulations allow nurses to prescribe they should do so only when they are acting within their individual expertise.

Patient group directions

All nurses, and indeed a number of other health professionals, can, within their NHS practice only, supply and administer specified prescription-only medicines within a patient group direction. In law, a patient group direction (formerly known as a group protocol) is essentially a delegation of authority under Section 58.2 (b) of the Medicines Act by an appropriate practitioner, usually a doctor, to another health professional, usually a nurse. Health Service Circular 2000/026 (NHS Executive 2000) and the Welsh equivalent, Chief Nursing Officer letter 2000/05 (National Assembly for Wales 2000) outline the scope and requirements of patient group directions and refer back to more detailed guidance issued under Health Service Circular 1998/051 (NHS Executive 1998b) (Chief Nursing Officer 98/4 in Wales (Welsh Office 1998)).

Accountability

The essence of being a professional is to have a recognised area of expertise requiring some formal qualification that, once obtained, gives to the holders of that qualification as a group discretion (within the law) as to how they practise. This does not mean that professionals, either individually or as a group, are unaccountable. On the contrary, all professionals are accountable to society as a whole, to the individuals whom they serve and to their professional body, and, if the professionals work within an organisation, to their employer.

Applying these general principles to nursing, there are usually three lines of accountability:

- Nurses will have a legal accountability to the courts both in criminal law and in civil law
- Nurses will have a professional accountability to the UKCC
- If employed, nurses will have a contractual accountability to their employer.

The areas of activity, which nurses will be accountable for, can be divided into three groups:

- Personal conduct
- Professional conduct
- Professional practice.

We are concerned here primarily with accountability and legal issues relating to professional practice (which are matters of civil law) of which nurse prescribing is one particular area.

Before leaving the general issue of accountability it is important to remember that all three of the bodies to which a nurse is accountable (the profession, the employer and the Court), will judge professional practice on similar criteria, that is, as to whether it is acceptable to professional peers. However, the standard of proof that each has to have in arriving at a judgement is different. If a nurse's professional practice were criticised, the employer is required only to have a reasonable belief that those criticisms are accurate, whereas a civil court must have proof on the balance of probabilities while a criminal court and the UKCC must be satisfied beyond a reasonable doubt. In theory therefore it could be quite correct in relation to the same allegation for an employer to discipline a nurse but for a civil court and the UKCC to dismiss the allegation. Similarly, a nurse could quite properly be disciplined by the employer and have damages awarded against him or her by a civil court and the allegations dismissed by a criminal court and the UKCC.

In practice, to date, it is rare for either an employer or the UKCC to take any action against a nurse or any other health professional on the basis of an isolated allegation of professional negligence having been proved. Employers and the UKCC are typically more proactive where there is a series of criticisms involving the same individual even if those criticisms have not been the subject of civil litigation.

This is speculation but it seems that, in the future, employers may become stricter with clinical staff primarily because of the development of increasingly well-defined clinical policies and procedures and the development of evidence-based medicine. In the past when clinical practice was less well defined the grounds for disciplinary action were consequently less clear cut. Nurses and other health professionals who do not follow explicit procedures and policies laid down by their employer in relation to clinical practice are in principle as open to disciplinary action as anyone else who fails to follow a reasonable instruction from an employer.

Accountability to the criminal courts

Health professionals are in the same position as anybody else in relation to the criminal law. It is rare for health professionals to be charged with serious criminal offences in connection with their care of patients. Generally criminal law requires that the offender not only performs the criminal act but also has the intention of performing that criminal act.

It is important to remember that the Medicines Act makes any infringement of that Act a criminal offence. Nurse prescribers, therefore, must be sure that they remain within the scope of nurse prescribing and the *Nurse Prescribers' Formulary*. If nurses are supplying and administering prescription-only medicines to patients outside the *Formulary* then that must be done within the scope of an appropriate patient group direction.

Accountability to the civil courts

The civil courts deal with clinical negligence claims. The principles followed in the civil courts, and particularly the principle established in the case of *Bolam* v. *Friern Hospital Management Committee* [1957] are central in the accountability of health professionals. NHS employees are indemnified for the cost of civil claims by their employer but it is otherwise for the individual to obtain appropriate professional indemnity insurance.

Briefly, to succeed in a claim for clinical negligence, the claimant has to prove, on the test of the balance of probabilities, three things:

1. That a duty of care existed between the Claimant and the Defendant. There is an established duty of care in law between health professionals and their patients. In law, a health professional does not have a duty of care to anyone who is not his or her patient but if a health professional voluntarily attends an individual (for example in helping an accident victim if the health professional happens to be in the vicinity) a health professional then takes on a duty of care for that individual. Ethically and professionally, however, it may be expected that health professionals will act as a 'Good Samaritan'.

2. That there was a breach of that duty. The courts will judge this by reference to what is known as the 'Bolam' test. In that case the Judge said:

   A doctor is not guilty of negligence if he has acted in accordance with a practice accepted as proper by a responsible body of medical men skilled in that particular art.

   It is important to emphasise that the expert opinion must be responsible. A subsequent case, *Bolitho* v. *City and Hackney Health Authority* [1993], underlined that existing professional practices had to be justifiable. It is no defence to show that others also followed unacceptable practice.

3. That damage has been caused to the Claimant as a result of that breach of the duty of care. This is what is called causation. It is important to remember that, even if the Claimant demonstrates a breach of the duty of care, liability is limited to the damage that the Claimant can prove probably resulted from that breach and if there is no damage then there is no liability.

There are two other principles of civil law that are important here. The first is the principle that a professional must not act outside his or her competence. The patient does not know the extent of the nurse's knowledge. The responsibility is on the nurse to act only within his or her expertise. The duty to act only within one's competence is likely to become even more crucial if nurse prescribing powers are broadened. The law may allow health professionals to prescribe a range of items but in practice the health professional can properly prescribe only those items within the range that fall within his or her expertise otherwise the prescribing is negligent.

Finally, the standard that the Courts expect is that of the reasonably competent practitioner. It is what lawyers call an 'objective' standard. That is to say that the standard does not vary because different individuals are carrying out the tasks. So far as nurse prescribing is concerned therefore, the same standard of competence will be expected of a nurse prescribing as a doctor prescribing that medication. That standard will be established by reference to the principle in the Bolam test, that is to say acceptability to a responsible group of professional peers.

Accountability to an employer

This is a matter of contract law, which will specifically depend on the detail of the individual contract of employment. However, as far as professional matters are concerned employers generally follow the approach of the civil courts. That is, they expect practice and conduct to be such as to be acceptable to a responsible body of professional peers. Increasingly employers have formal protocols and procedures relating to various aspects of clinical practice and health professionals may be obligated to follow their employers' guidelines.

Accountability to the UKCC

To practise as a nurse an individual must be registered with the UKCC. In its disciplinary role the UKCC can consider the practice and conduct of individual nurses. Once again the test of acceptable practice is as laid down in Bolam. The UKCC will of course also consider matters of personal conduct including criminal acts. The UKCC works to the standard of proof of the criminal courts, that is to say proof beyond a reasonable doubt but if a nurse's practice or conduct is found to be unacceptable then he or she may be suspended or removed from the nursing register by the UKCC. The UKCC has issued written guidelines on the administration of medicines (2000).

Other legal issues relevant to nurse prescribing

There are four other legal issues that are particularly relevant to nurse prescribing:

- Consent
- Record keeping
- Vicarious liability
- Product liability

Consent

A patient is not obliged to receive treatment. The responsibility on the health professional is to try to ensure that the patient understands both the nature of the treatment which is in prospect and also the relevant advantages and risks of undergoing that treatment. If a patient has not consented to treatment that is undertaken the patient could pursue a claim for battery against the health professional although in practice such a claim is perhaps unlikely unless it forms part of broader allegations of clinical negligence. However, an employer or the UKCC may nonetheless take action against any nurse who has treated a patient without the patient's consent.

Consent can be:

- *Implied:* for example consent for examination may be implied from a patient removing his shirt for the examination to be undertaken
- *Oral:* for example a patient agreeing verbally to have his wrist X-rayed

- *Written:* for example a patient signing a consent form for an operation.

In law all these types of consent are valid. The advantage of written consent is that the signed document provides clear evidence of what was agreed by the patient. The question of when written consent needs to be obtained should be considered in the light of the Bolam principle as to what is acceptable professional practice.

Provided the health professional is satisfied that the patient has the mental capacity to allow a sufficient understanding of the nature and extent of the treatment proposed consent can be obtained from any patient over the age of 16. If a patient over 18 does not have the capacity to consent then in law the responsibility reverts to the health professional to act in the best interests of his or her patient. As a matter of good practice the health professional should consult with close relatives or friends and if possible obtain their assent but the final decision on the patient's treatment is one for the health professional. No one can consent to treatment for another adult although under certain sections of the Mental Health Act 1983 some treatment can be given without the patient's consent.

Consent for minors

As far as individuals aged under 18 are concerned, those aged 16 and above are able to consent to their own treatment because of the provisions of the Family Law Reform Act 1969. A patient under 16 years can give a valid consent to treatment provided he or she is 'Gillick competent' (*Gillick* v. *West Norfolk and Wisbech Area Health Authority* [1985]). That is to say the health professional is satisfied that the patient is of sufficient understanding and intelligence to enable him or her to understand fully what is proposed. While only one consent is needed in law, unless treatment is required urgently or there is an issue of confidentiality between the minor and those with parental authority, and as a matter of good practice, it would be preferable to obtain also the agreement of an individual with parental responsibility to treatment of a minor. With unmarried parents it is usually only the mother who has parental responsibility, unless the father has specifically obtained it by applying to a Court or by formal agreement with the mother. Parental consent must be exercised in the best interest of the child and the health professional's duty is to act in the best interest of the patient even if that does not accord with parental wishes.

Consent in emergencies

In an emergency, when it is not possible to obtain consent in time, the health professional can act in the patient's best interest if that is necessary to preserve life or to secure improvement or prevent deterioration in the patient's condition. However, the patient's best interest must take into account any known views of the patient as well as the health professional's assessment.

'Informed' consent

For a patient's consent to be valid the patient must have an adequate knowledge of the purpose, nature and risks of the treatment including the likelihood of success and any alternatives to it as well as having pointed out any advantages or risks which in the particular circumstances of the patient are likely to be relevant.

Record keeping

The importance of good record keeping for health professionals can hardly be overemphasised. The UKCC (1998) issues specific guidance in relation to record keeping. Record keeping should be to an acceptable professional standard. Good practice linked with adequate record keeping should place the health professional in the position of being able to refute any criticism effectively.

Vicarious liability

In a sense, vicarious liability is the reverse of accountability to an employer because it makes the employer liable for the actions of the employee. Health Service Guidance 1996/48 (DoH 1996) defines the arrangements so far as clinical staff directly employed by NHS bodies are concerned. In essence, clinical staff are indemnified in respect of their NHS duties by their employing NHS authority. That means that even if there were successful civil proceedings for damages against an individual member of staff the employing authority would pay those damages and the circular also provides that employing authorities should not seek to recover damages from an individual member of staff. Clinical staff not so employed including GPs and their staff, should have appropriate professional indemnity insurance which is available either from one of the medical defence organisations, professional bodies or from commercial insurers.

Product liability

Broadly, if equipment or medication is not used in line with the manufacturer's instructions then the manufacturer may escape liability in respect of any failure in the product. In the context of nurse prescribing this means that care needs to be taken with product licences and also of manufacturer's guidance in relation for example to the storage of medication. There are of course many occasions when medication is quite properly used outside its product licence particularly in paediatrics, but health professionals should only do this knowingly when they are satisfied there is good reason for it.

Conclusion

The principles of accountability and law outlined above apply to nurse prescribing as to other areas of professional nursing practice. Nurse prescribing itself though is a very precisely defined activity restricted to certain categories of nurses employed within the NHS who have undergone the required further training. Nurse prescribing is different and distinct from the supply and administration of medicines under a patient group direction.

Professional accountability should not be as much of a problem for nurses as it might at first appear. Although nurses are accountable in a number of different directions, all those to whom they are accountable expect them to behave and work to similar criteria.

To avoid criticism from any of those to whom nurses are accountable they should:

● Behave generally in ways that are acceptable and within social norms

● Ensure that their professional conduct and practice is such as to be acceptable to their professional peers – the more mainstream an individual's professional practice is the easier it will be to defend in the event of any criticism

● Act professionally only within their competence

● Maintain a good standard of record keeping so that any criticism can be defended.

NOTE: This chapter reflects the position in England according to the state of the law as at 1 August 2001. While legislation permits nurse prescribing and patient group directions throughout the United Kingdom the extent to which nurses may prescribe and patient group directions may be used is a matter for each of the separate administrations in England, Wales, Scotland and Northern Ireland.

Further reading

Jones, M.A. (1996) *Medical Negligence*. 2nd edn. Sweet & Maxwell, London.
Powers, N. and Harris, N. (2000) *Clinical Negligence*. Butterworths, London.

References

Bolam v. *Friern Hospital Management Committee* [1957] 2 All ER 118.
Bolitho v. *City and Hackney Health Authority* [1993] 4 Medical Law Reports 381.
DoH (1996) *Arrangements for Handling Clinical Negligence Claims Against NHS Staff.* Health Services Guidance (HSG) 1996/48. DoH, London.
Gillick v. *West Norfolk and Wisbech Area Health Authority* [1985] 3 All ER 402.
NHS Executive (1998a) *Nurse Prescribing*. Health Service Circular (HSC) 1998/232. DoH, London.
NHS Executive (1998b) *Report on the Supply and Administration of Medicines Under Group Protocols*. Health Service Circular (HSC) 1998/051 21 April 1998. NHSE, Leeds. [Welsh Office (1998) Chief

Nursing Officer 98/4 *Review of Prescribing, Supply and Administration of Medicines.*]

NHS Executive (2000) *Patient Group Directions.* Health Service Circular (HSC) 2000/026 DoH, London. [National Assembly for Wales (2000) *Review of Prescribing, Supply and Administration of Medicines – Sale, Supply and Administration of Medicines by Health Professionals under Patient Group Directions.* Welsh *Nurse Prescribing Circular* Chief Nursing Officer letter 2000/05 – 22nd December 2000.]

UKCC (1998) *Guidelines for Records and Record Keeping.* UKCC, London.

UKCC (2000) *Guidelines for the Administration of Medicines.* UKCC, London.

Assessment and evaluation in nurse prescribing

Jennifer L. Humphries

The focus of this chapter is to consider some of the principles of assessment and evaluation in the nursing care of patients and clients. Nurse prescribing has the potential to allow prescribing nurses to contemplate their assessment and evaluation approaches, and the chapter will examine some theoretical perspectives and consider how these apply when nurses are prescribers. Throughout the chapter the term 'nurse' includes nurses, midwives and health visitors.

Assessment

The assessment of patients and clients often involves the collection of large amounts of information that the nurse uses to determine health status and needs, and to plan appropriate care. Nurse prescribers use the same skills and strategies as used prior to qualification, but the assessment now has the added dimension of a possible nurse prescription. In some circumstances, the nurse will be able to anticipate a prescribing episode; for example, a nurse administering vaccinations may routinely write a prescription for paracetamol to reduce post-immunisation pyrexia. Other prescribing may depend upon the features that arise during an encounter and will result in a prescription being generated immediately, for example a nurse prescribing clotrimazole for an infant with nappy-area thrush. A third type of prescribing incident is a combination of the first two. In this situation, the nurse has previously given care or offered advice and is returning to reassess, with the anticipation of prescribing if the original programme or strategy has been unsuccessful. For example, a nurse may provide dietary advice for constipation and later prescribe a laxative.

The question, then, is whether prescribing becomes paramount in the patient/client assessment. The short answer is that it does not. A nurse does not cease being a nurse, a health visitor, or a midwife when he or she becomes a prescriber, and, for many current prescribers, writing a prescription remains a rare event. Assessment of the patient or client is as before but, should certain types of treatment included in the NPF be required, the nurse is able to supply them by writing a prescription.

Models of care

In assessing patients and clients, nurses adopt a method of collecting and organising the information to plan and implement care. A variety of models is available to assist the practitioner in determining patient/client health status, identifying problems or needs and making decisions about the care delivery. Cormack and Reynolds (1992, p. 1473) describe a model as:

> A statement which causes nurses to perceive patients, their environment and their health/illness status in a specific way. It influences the way in which nurses understand and interpret the aetiology of pathology and of nursing needs, how these needs are identified, and how appropriate nursing intervention is selected to meet those needs, and the subsequent evaluation of that intervention.

Some models are developed specifically for use by nurses, while others have been adapted from, for example, psychology or health promotion. Most models currently used by nurses, whether of nursing or borrowed from another discipline, are likely to be suitable for nurse prescribing. However, prescribing is a new realm of nursing practice and affords practitioners the ideal opportunity for appraising existing frameworks or models used in current practice.

Sbaih (1997) suggests that the use of a framework for care should provide:

- a common starting place for nurses and clients
- a guide for the development of questions by the nurse, client and family to gain information

- a basis for participation and collaboration
- an opportunity for reflection on care-giving.

These points are useful for nurse prescribers who wish critically to evaluate the pertinence of a current model for nurse prescribing or to consider the suitability of a new approach.

Nursing knowledge and skills in assessing patients and clients

It is evident that a diagnosis has to have been reached in order to prescribe. Some nurses may initially feel uncomfortable with this since diagnosing has traditionally been the domain of doctors. Further examination, however, shows that diagnosis is indeed already part of nursing practice. Consider first that nursing diagnosis is well established and forms the basis of episodes of care. Nurses have the skills to assess, plan, implement and subsequently evaluate nursing intervention.

Second, nursing intervention, whether in the community or hospital, frequently involves giving advice about prescribed medication. In the community setting, following assessment, nurses often advise clients and patients about over-the-counter preparations. A survey by *Community Nurse* magazine (Anderson 1995) found that 73 per cent of practice nurse respondents were involved in a clinic where they influenced changes of patients' medication, and 93 per cent of health visitor respondents regularly gave advice about over-the-counter medication. Advice about medication is sometimes little more than providing the name of a product, but it often involves detailed information about the use, effects and storage of the drug. Thus nurses' contribution to patient education concerning medication is as relevant in patient care as the ability to administer medication (Latter et al. 2001). Clearly, this part of practice is health education; it is advice based on a theoretical and practical knowledge of the preparation and on professional experience of product use by other patients and clients.

Third, nurses are always accountable for their practice; prescribing does not make a nurse more accountable. Prescribing, rather than advising on a product, may be less risky for both nurse and patient. The nurse prescriber may ultimately have more, rather than less, control over the episode of care, and the patient or client may arguably receive more comprehensive information about a nurse-prescribed product, because it is provided in the context of the whole assessment process, than if he or she went to the pharmacist. The likelihood of fragmented care is reduced, and the patient may feel that a prescribed item is of more value than one bought from the pharmacy.

Finally, the diagnosis of conditions within nursing practice is not new; indeed, when nurse prescribing was first advocated, it was noted that district nurses were requesting prescriptions for some products to treat certain conditions (DHSS 1986). A study by Kendrick et al. (2000) identified that health visitors are diagnosing and advising on a range of childhood illnesses and nurse practitioners have long been recognised as being involved in advanced nursing practice that requires complex decision-making skills in respect of assessment, diagnosis and treatment (Brykczynski 1991). The government specifically acknowledges the skills of nurses in some diagnoses: NHS Direct, the service from which members of the public are able to seek information and advice about health and medical conditions, is staffed by nurses. The nurse-led walk-in centres and minor injury units involve nurses making diagnoses, as do some of the structures that are incorporated into the PMS (personal medical services) schemes.

Assessing patients and clients often results in a medical diagnosis that, before nurse prescribing, meant that the planning and implementation of patient care included a referral to the doctor. Now, however, if a nurse is a prescriber, the assessment of the same patient or client resulting in the same diagnosis means the nursing intervention can be one of prescribing rather than referral.

If nurses are to prescribe, they clearly have to be competent to do so. Training is important and most practitioners will feel suitably equipped to prescribe in their role following this. Having the legal authority to prescribe does not mean that the nurse should always do so, there may be those practitioners who do not feel sufficiently skilled to prescribe certain preparations. Clearly, the more experience a professional has in dealing with a condition, the more confident he or she is likely to feel about prescribing treatment for that condition. For example, although nurses can prescribe from a wide range of dressing products, only certain prescribers will possess the necessary skills and knowledge of wound care to do so. Similarly some practitioners may have extensive and up-to-date knowledge of scabies, while others may have had little experience of the condition and may prefer to refer the patient, even though he or she can legally prescribe appropriate lotions. It may be that only when faced with a particular condition do nurses become aware that a lack of recent experience has reduced their confidence in diagnosing and treating. The obvious solution in the immediate situation is to refer to a colleague who does feel competent, be it another nurse or a doctor, but in the longer term it can be something about which a nurse prescriber may feel compelled to gain additional knowledge and experience. Much will depend on the context in which the professional works, and a community, practice or workload profile can serve as a useful method of determining the needs of the population relating specifically to prescribing. Assessing the needs of populations and communities may establish the prevalence of, for example, head lice and a current lack of knowledge of the condition would prevent nurse prescribers from fulfilling not just their prescribing role but also a public health function. Practitioners have a professional responsibility to ensure competence before prescribing, and the presentation of clearly defined information can serve as a tool to ask for additional training. Updating on aspects of pharmacology may be required before a nurse feels competent to prescribe some of the preparations in the NPF (Courtney and Butler 1998).

All nurses use their knowledge and skills in assessing patients and regularly make decisions about the need for patients or clients to consult a doctor. A prescribing practitioner maintains this option. The ability to prescribe does not mean that it will always be the intervention of choice. Most practitioners will continue to use their skills to identify and define the patients' complaints and discriminate these from other possible conditions. As always, referral to a medical colleague for assessment and possible treatment continues to be an alternative.

Clinical decision-making

Prescribing assessment is part of the whole assessment procedure but, for some new prescribers, the use of skills and knowledge in making the clinical decision may become explicit, being a conscious decision to use the knowledge and practise the skills. Luker and Kenrick (1992) examined the sources of influence on the clinical decisions of community nurses in the context of nurse prescribing. The results of the small exploratory study, undertaken before the nurse prescribing pilot, indicated that even highly skilled practitioners were often unable to articulate the source of their knowledge for clinical decisions. This is not a new phenomenon, Benner (1984) suggesting that expert practitioners regard situations holistically, drawing on experiences and being unconsciously guided by intuition and 'gut feelings'. Luker and Kenrick (1992) acknowledge that experiential knowledge may be scientific knowledge that has been integrated by the practitioner and reclassified. These authors do not devalue clinical experience, although they do suggest that it may be used at the expense of science. Moreover, they note that it is nurses' lack of ability to articulate the source of their knowledge that may impede their credibility and inhibit the transmission of the knowledge to new practitioners.

Research looking at decision-making in the context of nurse prescribing (Luker et al. 1998) found that a significant influence on prescribing was the nurse's own expertise. The authors of the study note that while there is a move towards evidence-based practice, nurses continue to use experiential knowledge, for example previous experience of conditions and knowledge of the patient/client. A variety of factors will impact on the nurse prescriber's decision-making, often, as noted by Peate (1996), dependent on context. Scientific evidence is just one element in the processes employed by practitioners in clinical decision-making (Mead 2000) and prescribing decisions will be based on numerous factors. The crucial feature is the skill of nurses in synthesising these within each episode of care: as Schober (1993) notes of the relationship between nursing theory and nursing knowledge:

> Nursing is essentially a practice discipline, but the quality of practice depends upon attitudes, knowledge and abilities for effective care. The way nurses use knowledge and apply theory will influence their approach to nursing; sound decision-making depends upon using knowledge expertly.
>
> (p. 310)

Prescribing is just one way of providing nursing care, the decision to prescribe being ultimately that of the nurse. Brew (1997, p. 239) reminds us that nurses need to be professionally and legally accountable for their actions and offers the following factors for consideration concerning nurse prescribing:

- The patient's circumstances, including current medication
- The patient's past medical history
- The patient's current and anticipated health status
- Thorough knowledge of the item to be prescribed, its therapeutic action, side-effects, dosage and interaction
- Thorough knowledge of alternatives to prescribing
- Frequency of use in a variety of circumstances.

Assessment allows the nurse to establish whether prescribing is the most appropriate intervention. Having determined this the prescriber is faced with prescribing the appropriate product. The National Prescribing Centre (1999) suggests nurses may find the mnemonic 2-WHAM useful:

W   –   Who is it for?
W   –   What are the symptoms?
H   –   How long have the symptoms been present?
A   –   Action taken so far?
M   –   Medication currently being taken?

Whenever possible, nurses involve patients in decisions about care, and prescribing is no different in this. Including patients or clients in assessing their health status and needs may be influential in encouraging concordance with the treatment prescribed. To ensure safe and effective prescribing, it is vital to assess current medication or treatment in order to guard against possible drug interactions. A variety of strategies may need to be employed to find out the information. People do not necessarily perceive medication bought from a supermarket as a drug and may offer information only about prescribed items. Asking to see products enables the nurse to determine the ingredients contained in some proprietary brands and affords an opportunity for health education, including discussing the storage and use of medicines and stressing the importance of using prescribed products only for the person named on the prescription and not for family or friends.

Determining previous medication and treatment is also essential since efficacy in the past can be significant in deciding specific products.

Evaluation

Evaluating the quality of health care is essential for all health professionals. The concept is not new: McIntyre (1995) cites Florence Nightingale as advocating the systematic collection of information to improve patient treatment. Various terms are used when discussing evaluation in health care, including 'clinical audit', 'quality initiatives' and 'measuring effectiveness'. Luker (1992) notes that evaluation is often referred to by other terms, for example 'appraisal' or 'assessment'. Many of the principles apply to the whole range of evaluation strategies. Essentially, the idea of nursing evaluation is to determine whether nursing intervention has been effective. If it has, it allows the principles employed to be repeated for the benefit of other patients and clients, and allows examples of good practice to be passed on to other practitioners so that their patients and clients can also profit. The evaluation of an activity shown not to be satisfactory prevents its repetition, and therefore this, too, ultimately results in improved patient care.

Evaluation is part of the nursing process and constitutes a cyclical activity. It is not always straightforward: some aspects of evaluation are informal, and there may be difficulty in isolating particular issues for evaluation since they may not be readily delineated from other parts of the care provided. An issue of relevance to community nursing is the often long-term nature of intervention, the impact not becoming apparent for months or years; even then, as a health promotion or disease prevention intervention, it can be difficult to measure. An independent prescribing activity, however, often offers nurses the opportunity for a more accelerated evaluation.

The evaluation of nursing intervention can range from the simple to the highly complex depending on what is being evaluated, and it is this point that is perhaps the crux of any evaluation scheme. It is essential to determine exactly what is being evaluated and to decide appropriate methods of collecting and analysing the information that will address the evaluation plan.

One manner of describing the mechanisms associated with evaluation is to divide the whole into three distinct arenas: structure, process and outcome (Donabedian 1980). In nurse prescribing, examples of structure would be the composition of the teams providing the prescribing care and the expertise of the staff. The process would be the delivery of the prescribing care, and the outcome would be the effectiveness of that care.

Structure evaluation

The main facets for structure of evaluation are likely to bring to the fore the expertise of the nurse who prescribes. This is interesting because the impetus behind nurse prescribing came from the premise that nurses had the expertise and were, in many cases, prescribing informally (DHSS 1986). Luker et al.'s (1997a) evaluation of the nurse prescribing pilot suggests that the content of the nurse prescribers' training course was good and adequately prepared the nurses for their role as prescribers. It has to be noted that just because nurses can prescribe, it does not mean that they will, and the prescribing nurses' view is that they would only prescribe if they had the necessary training and experience (Luker et al. 1997b).

Process evaluation

Within the episode of patient or client care, the evaluations of nursing activity and patient outcome are frequently integrated. For example, the effectiveness of a prescription for paracetamol (the outcome) can usually be determined very rapidly, but the prescription will not have been issued in isolation, and it is therefore vital that process evaluation is incorporated. The parents of a baby with post-immunisation pyrexia will also have been given advice about the care of the infant concerning clothing, fluids and handling. A patient with mild-to-moderate pain will have been given additional information about management that addresses the source of the pain. In both instances, the patient or client will have been told what to do if the problem persists in spite of the medication.

Thus the information supplied with the prescription is a vital aspect of the role of the nurse prescriber, since incorrect usage can result in the treatment being ineffective. Patients and clients require clear and concise information about the items prescribed; they should be told about the effects of the medication or treatment and how soon these may be expected. Some preparations have side-effects, and, although most are rare and/or mild, information about these can assist patients in discriminating between these and a severe adverse reaction and can help to ensure that the treatment is not stopped prematurely. Clear instructions about when and how to take the medication, any special precautions and what to do if they have any concerns should be given verbally and, if necessary, in written form.

Outcome evaluation

Outcome evaluation may initially seem to be the most obvious form of evaluation for nurse prescribers. Was the prescription effective? Has the headache gone, the constipation resolved, the wound healed, the infection cleared? Its appeal is evident because what health professionals ultimately want to know is what the results of the intervention were for the patient; according to McIntyre (1995), many would consider outcome to be the most relevant indicator of quality of care.

Despite its immediate attraction, outcome evaluation can be complex to measure. Patient outcome is notoriously difficult to link to, or separate from, clinical (nursing or medical) intervention. Remember the old adage 'the operation was a success but the patient died'. This problem is compounded by the nature of community nursing, because, unlike in a hospital setting where care is provided on a 24-hour basis, hands-on or face-to-face contact occupies a very small part of the care package. So many other factors impinge on the intervention that it is very difficult to ascertain how far the outcome relates to the process. The complexity of an apparently simple intervention is not confined to nurse prescribers, so prescribing nurses are not subjected to new dilemmas about appropriate ways of evaluating nursing intervention and the link to patient outcome. However, nurse prescribing can add a slightly different dimension. Non-prescribing nurses offer advice about medication, for example in the case of pyrexia or pain, they may recommend paracetamol from the pharmacy or often from the home medicine cabinet, so evaluation of the intervention is thus already part of the care provided. A nurse prescriber, however, may evaluate the appropriateness of writing the prescription and, on reflection, may question whether the patient or client should have been advised to buy the product. Financial and social circumstances are likely to impinge on the decision to prescribe (Luker et al. 1997a, 1998), and a review could result in alterations to existing practice.

Patient/client satisfaction

When attempting to evaluate effectiveness, it is imperative to decide not only what to evaluate, but also whose judgement is to be used. In the area of nurse prescribing, it is possible that the nurse and patient may view the situation differently. Take, for example, the patient with a leg wound who would have preferred a different dressing despite the rational and careful explanation by the district nurse, or the mother of a constipated toddler who views the detailed health education given by the health visitor as being of less use than a prescription for a laxative. Patient satisfaction is important, and some nurse prescribers may choose to modify their treatment if they consider that the patient is more likely to comply and/or has great faith in the product, especially if there is little or no difference between the two treatments. There are undoubtedly those patients and clients who have ultimate confidence in professional expertise; many nurses know of individuals and families who would not go to the pharmacy for an over-the-counter preparation but who would adhere rigorously to the instructions that accompany a prescription. Professional judgement is part of a nurse's role, and the decision to prescribe rests with the prescriber. The crucial aspect is whether the prescriber has a rational justification for the decision.

Clinical audit

Clinical audit is a formal and systematic analysis of practice that includes aspects of the quality of care provided, procedures, the use of resources and the resulting outcome. Audit is an ideal procedure for use with nurse prescribing because it enables the prescribing to be analysed objectively as a specific area of practice.

Another advantage of audit for nurse prescribing is that it frequently involves standard-setting whereby specific and measurable criteria are identified for detailed examination. Ideally, all staff who are to participate in the audit should agree the standard. Setting standards is often based on previous research, and, in this, nurse prescribers will initially have little British nurse prescribing evidence of practice to which to refer. This should not deter nurse prescribers from attempting audit from the outset since evidence of good practice is an acceptable alternative. The importance of keeping up to date with developments in nursing is essential. Information about research and practice that may be applicable in the field of nurse prescribing can be found in national and international nursing journals and obtained from professional nursing bodies. A critical analysis of the prescribing activity of other professional groups, such as GPs, may prove useful to nurse prescribers. This information may be gained informally from GP colleagues who are willing to share their personal experiences or from medical publications.

Although nurse prescribing in other countries may not be directly transferable to British experience, useful comparisons may be made to develop prescribing practice. Shepherd et al. (1996) note that American studies on nurse prescribing suggest that financial savings on administrative overheads have been made. They also note that, in Australia, nurses have been particularly active in developing policy in the quality use of medicines.

Comparing prescribing practice with agreed standards should also identify other issues for audit and allow the cycle to begin again.

Clinical supervision

One of the recommendations of the evaluation of nurse prescribing is that a model of clinical supervision is necessary to ensure the development of effective nursing practice (Luker et al. 1997a).

Swain (1995) suggests that clinical supervision is now an established aspect of professional development for nurses, midwives and health visitors. The idea of clinical supervision in caring for patients and clients is not new, although permeation of the principle received considerable impetus through *A Vision for the Future* (NHSME 1993). Clinical supervision is described in this document as:

> A term used to describe a formal process of professional support and learning which enables individual practitioners to develop knowledge and competence, assume responsibility for their own practice and enhance consumer protection and the safety of care in complex clinical situations. It is central to the process of learning and to the expansion of the scope of practice and should be seen as a means of encouraging self-assessment and analytical and reflective skills.
>
> (p. 15)

The intention of clinical supervision is therefore to enable practitioners to reflect on practice in a creative and supportive environment, allowing an opportunity for learning and professional development. Clinical supervision is also about ensuring high-quality care for patients and clients. Although Butterworth et al. (1997) suggest that there are a number of devotees of clinical supervision among British nurses, they acknowledge that the impact on patient care and the benefits for professionals are not well demonstrated by research.

As nurse prescribing is a relatively new venture, the processes involved in clinical supervision should be documented in order to enable subsequent prescribers to benefit. Some nurses may feel that the change of status to nurse prescriber is barely noticeable, that the ability to prescribe is simply a legitimisation of existing practice anyway. However, anecdotal evidence from nurse prescribing students is supported by the findings of the evaluation study (Luker et al. 1997a) that new prescribers are highly aware of their new role. There are bound to be some uncertainties for newly qualified prescribers, and advice and support are essential. While the anxiety about writing prescriptions may be shortlived, it should not be belittled, and clinical supervision can provide practitioners with a way of working through the anxieties so that confidence in clinical practice and prescribing can develop.

Evaluating personal development

Nurses are increasingly being confronted with a variety of strategies that assist them to evaluate their own clinical expertise and professional development. The mandatory requirement from the UKCC (1997) obliges every nurse, midwife and health visitor to keep an up-to-date profile of his or her professional development. As well as being a record of learning and achievement, the profile can be useful in encouraging practitioners to reflect on their experiences and can also help to link theory and practice. For some, the training to become a nurse prescriber may be the first formal undertaking of study for some time. It can provide a catalyst for the reflection of current practice and encourage an elaboration of the processes of reflection to encompass prescribing. Nurse prescribers may find other methods of encouraging reflection useful, for example describing experiences to colleagues and peers, as in case presentations or significant incident discussions in both formal and informal situations. The educational preparation and training will encourage prescribers to assess their own progress in prescribing, and it is crucial that nurse prescribers constantly review their expertise and competence. Existing local practices and policies can allow the incorporation of prescribing evaluation, for example nursing team meetings, managerial meetings, individual performance review, health care team meetings and local meetings of professional associations.

Documentation

Record keeping is an integral part of nursing practice (UKCC 1998), contributing to, and assisting with, the whole of the nursing process, from assessment through to evaluation. It provides information about the patient and his or her nursing needs as well as satisfying legal requirements (Anderson 2000). Documentation in relation to prescribing is rigorous; it is not only nursing and patient-held notes but also, in many cases, medical notes that need to be updated on any prescribed products. Since nurse prescribers have to ensure accurate recording of their prescribing, there is great potential in the area of audit and in contributing to research about prescribing. Toms (1992) proposes that district nurses do not always place sufficient emphasis on record keeping, yet, as she notes, it can provide an encouraging record of nursing skills. Luker (1992) supports this view stating that 'the only area of a community health nurse's work which can readily be monitored is her record keeping' (p. 186). Dion (2001) takes the argument further by noting that maintaining accurate records can function as a safeguard for nurse prescribers in respect of proving professional ability and safe prescribing practice should any allegation arise that challenges these. Nurse prescribers need also to provide detail of the information given to the patient concerning management of the condition and the product prescribed. In some cases a nurse may make the decision not to prescribe, perhaps advising a GP consultation or an over-the-counter preparation. Documentation can allow the nurse to appraise prescribing decisions and offers a useful impetus for personal professional reflection.

Conclusion

This chapter has discussed the skills and expertise of nurses who are assessing and evaluating patient care in the context of nurse prescribing. Various strategies and ideas have been put forward that illustrate the essential sameness to practice without the ability to prescribe. The chapter has also recognised that nurse prescribing presents an ideal opportunity for nurses to review their existing practice, examine current knowledge and competence and reflect on their own personal and professional development.

References

Anderson, P. (1995) Your role in prescribing. *Community Nurse*, **1**(11): 20–2.

Anderson, E.E. (2000) Issues surrounding record keeping in district nursing practice. *British Journal of Community Nursing*, **5**(7): 352–6.

Benner, P (1984) *From Novice to Expert: Excellence and Power in Clinical Nursing Practice*. Addison-Wesley, Reading, MA.

Brew, M. (1997) Nurse prescribing. In Burley, S., Mitchell, E.E., Melling, K., Smith, M., Chilton, S. and Crumplin, C. (eds) *Contemporary Community Nursing*. Arnold, London, pp. 229–43.

Brykczynski, K. (1991) Judgement strategies for coping with ambitious clinical situations encountered in primary health care. *Journal of American Academic Nurse Practitioners*, **3**(2): 79–84.

Butterworth, T., Jeacock, J., Carson, J. and White, E. (1997) Clinical supervision: A hornet's nest or honey pot? *Nursing Times*, **93**(44): 27–9.

Cormack, D.F.S. and Reynolds, W. (1992) Criteria for evaluating the clinical and practical utility of models used by nurses. *Journal of Advanced Nursing*, **17**: 1472–8.

Courtney, M. and Butler, M (1998) Nurse prescribing – the knowledge base. *Nursing Times*, **94**(1): 40–2.

DHSS (1986) *Neighbourhood Nursing: A Focus for Care* (Cumberlege Report). HMSO, London.

Dion, X. (2001) Record keeping and nurse prescribing: an issue for concern? *British Journal of Community Nursing*, **6**(4): 193–8.

Donabedian, A. (1980) *Explorations in Quality Assessment and Monitoring*. Health Administration Press Vol.: *The Definition of Quality and Approaches to its Assessment*. Ann Arbor, Michigan.

Kendrick, D., Young, A. and Futers, D. (2000) The diagnosis and management of acute childhood illness: is there a role for health visitors? *Journal of Advanced Nursing*, **32**(6): 1492–8.

Latter, S., Ryecroft-Malone, J., Yerrrell, P. and Shaw, D. (2001) Nurses' educational preparation for a medication role: findings from a national survey. *Nurse Education Today*, **21**: 143–54.

Luker, K. (1992) Evaluating practice. In Luker, K. and Orr, J. (eds) *Health Visiting. Towards Community Health Nursing*. Blackwell: Oxford, pp. 159–90.

Luker, K.A. and Kenrick, M. (1992) An exploratory study of the sources of influence on the clinical decisions of community nurses. *Journal of Advanced Nursing*, **17**: 457–66.

Luker, K.A., Austin, L., Hogg, C., Willock, J., Wright, K., Ferguson, B., Jenkins-Clark, S. and Smith, K. (1997a) Evaluation of Nurse Prescribing Final Report: Executive Summary. Unpublished Report.

Luker, K.A., Austin, L., Willock, J., Ferguson, B. and Smith, K. (1997b) Nurses' and GPs' views of the *Nurse Prescribers' Formulary*. *Nursing Standard*, **11**(22): 33–8.

Luker, K.A., Hogg, C., Austin, L., Ferguson, B. and Smith, K. (1998) Decision making: the context of nurse prescribing. *Journal of Advanced Nursing*, 27: 657–65.

McIntyre, N. (1995) Evaluation in clinical practice: problems, precedents and principles. *Journal of Evaluation in Clinical Practice*, 1(1): 5–13.

Mead, P. (2000) Clinical guidelines: promoting clinical effectiveness or a professional minefield? *Journal of Advanced Nursing*, 31(1): 110–16.

National Prescribing Centre (1999) Signposts for prescribing nurses – general principles of good prescribing. *Prescribing Nurse Bulletin*, 1(1): 1–4.

NHS Management Executive (1993) *A Vision for the Future*. DoH, London.

Peate, I, (1996) How nurses make decisions regarding patient medication. *British Journal of Nursing*, 5(7): 417–18, 435–7.

Sbaih, L. (1997) Models of care. In Skidmore, D. (ed.) *Community Care: Initial training and Beyond*. Arnold, London, pp. 75–103.

Schober, J. (1993) Frameworks for nursing practice. In Hinchcliff, S.M., Norman, S.E. and Schober, J.E. (eds) *Nursing Practice and Health Care* (2nd edn). Arnold, London, pp. 300–27.

Shepherd, E., Rafferty, A.M. and James, V. (1996) Prescribing the boundaries of nursing practice: Professional regulation and nurse prescribing. *NT Research*, 1(6): 465–78.

Swain, G. (1995) *Clinical Supervision: The Principles and Process*. Health Visitors Association, London.

Toms, E.C. (1992) Evaluating the quality of patient care in district nursing. *Journal of Advanced Nursing*, 17: 1489–95.

UKCC (1997) *PREP and You*. UKCC, London.

UKCC (1998) *Guidelines for Records and Record Keeping*. UKCC, London.

5 Responsibilities of prescribing

Rosalyn Anderson

Individual responsibilities as a prescriber

All prescribers have a personal and legal responsibility to ensure that the most appropriate items are selected to meet the needs of the patient in a safe and cost-effective manner. The legal responsibility for prescribing always lies with the person who signs the prescription. It is dangerous to prescribe on the recommendation of a third party (even another health professional) if the prescriber has not seen the patient. By considering cost in relation to not only product selection, but also quantities prescribed, the prescriber should demonstrate financial responsibility. This should only be considered after the needs of the patient have been identified, when selection between alternative products with a similar action, but different cost, may be an option. Cost should never be the primary consideration.

The prescriber has a responsibility to the pharmacist to ensure that prescriptions are unambiguous. Although pharmacists have traditionally been expected to translate poorly written prescriptions, this is not acceptable and is fraught with dangers.

Clinical governance and the nurse prescriber

The intention of clinical governance is, 'to be the main vehicle for continuously improving the quality of patient care' (Scally and Donaldson 1998). In all primary care groups and trusts there should be a health professional with 'clinical governance' as their remit and responsibility. To this end they will work with the primary care team to ensure that through various mechanisms, including clinical audit, patient care is of optimal quality. Regular team meetings to discuss 'best practice' in relation to nurses' new responsibilities should enhance the prescribing process for everyone and encourage evidence-based practice, while discouraging an anecdotal approach to product choice. It is also essential that accurate and comprehensive clinical record keeping be maintained, identified as a major component of clinical governance in a Health Service Circular on this topic (HSC 1999/065). Records should include the reasons for product choices and show a logical approach to any change in treatment.

Security of prescriptions

Blank prescriptions should be regarded as blank cheques. Prescribers should never leave prescriptions unattended during a consultation. Prescriptions should be locked up when not in use and should not be left in a car.

Prescribers should always ensure that they use the appropriately pre-printed prescription, with correct identifiers, to ensure that it is attributed and costed correctly. Practice nurse prescriptions are coloured differently from those of community nurses and health visitors, and each trust or practice is provided with individually identifiable prescriptions for all staff.

Prescription-writing requirements

For every professional involved in prescription writing and interpretation, the safety of the patient is paramount. While there are legal requirements concerning the essential aspects of a prescription, there are additional recommendations to ensure that the pharmacist can accurately interpret the prescriber's wishes, check the doses prescribed, counsel patients appropriately and provide usable packs and patient leaflets. If any information, such as age, is omitted, this process becomes more difficult and more time consuming. Although the age of a child can be checked with the parent or guardian, other omissions may lead to considerable inconvenience for the patient if the prescriber has to be contacted by the pharmacist in order to clarify essential information. The following should be noted:

- a separate prescription must be written for each patient. In other words, nurses cannot prescribe a bulk pack of head lice lotion to treat a family
- all prescriptions must be computer printed or written in ink
- the prescriber must sign and date the prescriptions in ink
- the prescriber must sign and date any alterations in ink
- the date of birth must be stated.

Prescriptions must also include:

- the full name of the drug, dressing or appliance without the use of abbreviations, using the generic name where practicable. The brand name should be used for dressings and appliances to avoid the possibility of patients receiving an inappropriate product or even receiving a different product each time. Accurate patient medication records in pharmacies should help to identify previously issued products in order to update practice records and pharmacists can be consulted if details are unclear
- the strength and relevant identifying factors, such as the sizes of dressings and catheters
- the dose and frequency where possible
- directions in English with no abbreviations
- the minimum dose intervals for drugs that can be taken only when needed, for example 'not more than every 6 hours'
- the quantity required, with consideration of the pack size
- the quantities stated as follows:
  - less than 1 microgram: state in nanograms, for example 500 nanograms
  - less than 1 mg: state in micrograms, for example 500 micrograms
  - less than 1 g: state in milligrams, for example 500 mg
  - more than 1 g: state in grams, for example 1.5 g
  - for liquids: state the strength per ml, for example 250 mg/5 ml

ml, mg and g are acceptable abbreviations, but 'nanograms' and 'micrograms' should never be abbreviated.

Generic prescribing

As directed in the NPF, all products should, except where indicated otherwise, be prescribed by approved generic title as given in the *Formulary*. This title is usually the chemical name of the product, as distinct from the brand names that manufacturers use to market their own particular versions of that generic product. Some products are available only from one manufacturer and are given a brand name, but the generic description should still be used. Other products are produced in branded and generic forms, while some are only produced as generics.

Many generic tablets or capsules are produced by the manufacturer of the branded equivalent or by a subsidiary of that company. In such cases, the contents of both branded and generic products will be the same although the packaging will be different. Even when the generic manufacturer differs from the manufacturer of the brand, generic product colouring now usually matches the brand to avoid patient confusion. It is important for patients to be told that medicines will be generically prescribed, especially if they have previously received a branded product. There may be a more apparent difference between topical branded and generic products as the packaging may be markedly different. An example is Canesten cream, which patients may have received previously from the doctor, which is supplied in a tube and box differently coloured from those of the generic clotrimazole cream prescribed by nurses. Patients can be reassured that the contents of the tube contain exactly the same active ingredient and will treat the infection in the same way. Sometimes, even when a generic product is prescribed, the patient will receive a branded product. This is because it is often cheaper for some pharmacists and wholesalers to purchase the brand rather than the generic product. However, in such cases, the prescriber is credited with prescribing generically, and the practice or trust is charged accordingly.

Both branded and generic products have to comply with the stringent licensing requirements of the Medicines Control Agency, and patients can be reassured that all are equally safe in terms of the manufacturing process and the quality of the final product.

Parallel imports

These are medicinal products that are produced and packaged elsewhere in the EU and imported to the UK. The language of the exporting country is often apparent on the packaging, but none of the patient instructions should be in any language other than English. These products are often issued against generic prescriptions as, paradoxically, it is cheaper for the pharmacist to do this than to dispense a product manufactured and packaged in the UK. Patients can be reassured that these imported products must comply with the same high licensing standards that apply to products made in this country.

Additives or excipients in medicinal products or appliances

It is important to consider that certain patients may experience allergies to additives in medicines and other preparations. These components may differ between generic and branded products and between appliances made by different manufacturers which may contain different plasticisers. A simple example is that some ointments and creams contain lanolin as a major emollient component, but this is for many patients a potent skin sensitiser. Allergies may appear when patients change brands or from brand to generic and although patients sometimes resist any change from established products, the possibility of genuine allergy should not be ignored. If allergy is suspected, manufacturers should be asked to assist in identifying potential sensitisers in their products so that these can be avoided in the future. Patients should be advised to carry information on any allergies, and notes and computer records should be clearly marked. Pharmacists can provide details on available cards/jewellery such as MedicAlert which patients can carry or wear in case of emergency.

In terms of additives to improve flavouring, some medicines contain sugar and others do not. Where a sugar-free form is available, this should always be selected to reduce the risk of dental caries in those who receive regular medication, particularly in liquid forms. Such preparations are identified in the NPF.

Influences on prescribing

All professionals with prescribing responsibility are subjected to external prescribing influences from advertisements, representatives, sponsored events, other professionals and even the public. Prescribers should ensure that they have adequate unbiased information to make prescribing decisions, without reference to any form of sponsored publication. They should also be aware of issues of relevance to the public, such as items under discussion in the media, in order to address public concerns or questions about items that they may prescribe. All prescribers are subject to great attention from pharmaceutical companies; nurse prescribers will be no exception. A practice policy should be drawn up in conjunction with all prescribers to detail the level of drug promotion that is acceptable, for example in relation to sponsored meetings, and to agree an appointment system for pharmaceutical representatives in order to reduce frustrations on both sides. However, the practice and the prescribers must remain in control of this situation and clinical governance issues must remain a major concern. Medicines must always be selected to meet patient need, avoiding non-evidence-based influence. The UKCC can provide guidance to prescribers on acceptability of nurse–industry links. Trusts generally have local guidance covering relationships between industry and health professionals. The Prescription Medicines Code Of Practice Authority is designed to regulate industry activities but certain NPF items, for example dressings, may fall outside such control.

Independent reference sources for prescribers

Easily accessible books

British National Formulary

The British Medical Association and the Royal Pharmaceutical Society of Great Britain jointly publish the *British National Formulary* (BNF). It is a readily available reference source that includes all the medicinal products available for prescribing in the UK and also identifies products with restrictions on prescribing, for example isotretinoin is available from hospital or specified retail pharmacies only. Appendix 8 of the BNF details urinary and stoma appliances and Appendix 9 shows wound management products. The BNF is updated and published every six months and contains the NPF. The NPF itself is only updated and published every two years. If nurses need information on BNF products they should always refer to the latest edition.

Drug Tariff

This is published monthly by the DoH and distributed to each GP and community pharmacist and on a rotational basis to community nursing teams. Doctors generally utilise this book to a small degree and could usefully pass on at least one practice copy to nursing teams. It gives prices and prescribing details, including pack sizes, for various NPF products. Familiarity with this publication facilitates its usefulness, and the user should remember the following locations:

- generic oral and topical preparations (creams, ointments) – Part VIII
- wound management products – Part IXA
- catheters – Part IXA
- other incontinence appliances – Part IXB
- stoma appliances – Part IXC.

Other independent sources of prescribing information

Although the BNF gives some comparative therapeutic information, more detail will often be required in order to make a prescribing decision. Continuing education should facilitate rational, evidence-based prescribing and should assist critical analyses of research papers and company literature. Comparative information on drugs and other prescribable items can be resourced from local, regional and national drug information centres. Local community pharmacists or primary care group/ trust prescribing advisers should be a useful starting point if information is required quickly. Nurse prescribers should also be aware of some specific information sources relevant to the NPF. These include the local continence adviser and stoma nurse, taking into account any sponsorship of such posts. There are also national associations such as patient support groups and various publications that can provide useful information on stoma and incontinence aids which can assist with the prescribing nurse's choice.

MeReC Bulletins

All general practices receive a regular drug information bulletin with separate editions for England (MeReC), Scotland (Medicines Resource) and Wales (WeMeReC). This covers different therapeutic topics, with the emphasis on prescribing, and often includes comparative cost information. In Northern Ireland, the publication *Drug Data* is produced by the Regional Drug Information Service and covers similar topics.

Nurse prescribers should ask to be added to appropriate mailing lists. The National Prescribing Centre has produced nurse prescribing bulletins on pain relief, wound care, constipation, incontinence, and on management of infestations (scabies, threadworms and headlice). It also has a useful Internet site (www.npc.co.uk).

Drug and Therapeutics Bulletin

This is produced monthly by the publishers of *Which?*, the consumer magazine, but is written by health professionals for use by prescribers. It is particularly useful for reviews of new products in order to help prescribers to determine their place in the therapeutic armoury. Some issues cover reviews of drug groups, and a review of back issues is recommended.

National Institute for Clinical Excellence

The National Institute for Clinical Excellence (NICE) co-ordinates clinical information development and availability throughout England and Wales, in addition to producing evaluations and prescribing guidelines for various therapies. A MeReC Briefing document supports the implementation of NICE guidance and a separate document includes the key elements of each NICE guidance shortly after official publication as a summary for health professionals. These are accessible via the NICE Internet site (www.nice.org.uk).

Local drug information bulletins

Prescribers should check with local drug information centres (usually based in the pharmacy departments of the acute trusts) on the availability of local information bulletins. These may include comparative information on new drugs or may review the place of established products or therapies, especially where these are popular with local consultants. It may be possible to ask for a particular topic, for example recommendations for the management of infestations or the selection of wound management products, to be covered.

Primary care prescribing bulletins

These are usually produced by pharmaceutical and/or medical advisers in health authorities or commissions. They usually address current issues of relevance to primary care prescribing and to the primary–secondary care interface. They may report on local trends in GP and nurse prescribing.

To prescribe or not?

This dilemma faces all prescribers many times throughout the day and is sometimes perceived as a way of ending a consultation. Such prescribing is often inappropriate, and patients may actually be more in need of time than a prescription.

Prescribers may also demonstrate sub-optimal prescribing in the following ways:

- giving in to patient pressure to prescribe either an inappropriate drug and/or for an inappropriate reason, for example antibiotics for a probable viral infection
- repeating prescriptions for long periods of time with inadequate patient review (see below)
- prescribing new products without supporting clinical information to illustrate their advantages over existing products

- prescribing expensive products when equally effective cheaper products are readily available
- prescribing outdated products because of an inadequate updating of clinical knowledge.

The prescriber should therefore approach the prescribing process by adopting the following aims of good prescribing (Barber 1995) to:

- maximise effectiveness
- minimise risks
- minimise costs
- respect patient choices.

If these are met by every prescription on every occasion, clinical governance will be firmly established.

In order to meet these aims, the prescriber must consider many factors. The following considerations should become second nature as the good prescribing habit becomes established:

- Current and past medical problem – is a current diagnosis confirmed?
- The impact of other factors, such as smoking and alcohol intake, and diet.
- Over-the-counter medicines that the patient may be using.
- Currently prescribed drug therapy and indications for each prescribed item.
- Is a new prescription essential?
- Can any drugs or preparations be cancelled before adding new therapy?
- Are the safest and most effective products in use?
- Has cost been considered or are cheaper, equally safe and effective products available?
- Are drugs appropriate for the age of the patient in terms of not only dose, but also ease of application or administration?
- Can the patient take the drug correctly or apply it correctly?

- Has the patient suffered allergies in the past?
- Does the product contain potential allergens?
- Are there any cautions or contraindications to drug therapy?
- Are there any potential interactions between products?
- For how long should the treatment be needed?
- How often should the patient be reviewed in order to monitor the effectiveness of therapy?
- How will the response/improvement be measured?
- What is the correct description for the item required? This is particularly important for stoma and incontinence appliances, and computer drug and appliance pick lists can be confusing.
- What is an appropriate quantity based on normal usage?

Prescribers must also be able to recognise personal limitations in order to enable appropriate referral to nursing or medical colleagues when the diagnosis is uncertain and the appropriate treatment unclear. When selecting products from the NPF, special attention should be paid to the clinical warning boxes, which make recommendations about the need to refer to a doctor for advice, for example before prescribing laxatives for children.

Side-effects, drug interactions, cautions and adverse reactions

Side-effects

Common side-effects are given within each product monograph in the BNF, but, for more detail, including those side-effects that occur rarely, the *Summary of Product Characteristics*, formerly the *Data Sheet Compendium*, can be consulted. This is available from the Association of the British Pharmaceutical Industry, but a copy should be available in every general practice. Prescribers should be familiar with common side-effects as patients will be interested in potential problems with therapy. It is often better to prepare patients for possible side-effects rather than to deal with their worried questions after they have read the patient information leaflet. Such leaflets are provided by manufacturers in each pack of prescribable medicines. If, however, prescribers specify quantities that do not relate to available pack size then this poses difficulties for pharmacists in issuing leaflets.

Drug interactions

Major interactions of clinical significance are given in some sections of the NPF, for example for aspirin, but not usually within therapeutic sections of the BNF. In this publication Appendix 1 must be consulted. GP and pharmacist computer systems provide interaction warnings but clinical significance may need clarification.

Over-the-counter medicines and herbal products may interact with prescribed medicines. St John's Wort is an example of a 'natural' product with the potential for numerous interactions with prescribed medication, including certain anti-depressants (SSRIs), triptans, digoxin and warfarin (*Current Problems in Pharmacovigilance* 2000). Prescribers should always question patients about the use of any non-prescribed products, before initiating new therapy. Additional information on such interactions can be obtained from pharmacists and drug information centres.

Cautions and contraindications

Prescribers should aim to minimise the occurrence of adverse reactions to drug therapy by careful consideration of the need for additional medication. In detailing the points for consideration before prescribing additional treatments, various patient problems, for example renal and hepatic impairments, have been highlighted that can cause difficulties with certain drug treatments. Some drugs, particularly some systemic therapies, may be totally contraindicated in such patients, but always consult a doctor if there are concerns about any items in the NPF. BNF Appendix 2 (liver disease) and Appendix 3 (renal impairment) provide useful information on drugs to be avoided completely and those for which a dosage reduction is permissible. BNF Appendices 4 (pregnancy) and 5 (breastfeeding) are also useful sources of information. The BNF lists contraindications to treatments within each drug category, and the NPF has the same format. 'Cautions' are given, which need to be taken into account before prescribing particular drugs. The clinical relevance of such 'cautions' in individuals will often need to be discussed with a doctor.

Reporting adverse drug reactions

All prescribers have an extremely important role to play in the reporting of adverse drug reactions. In the UK, a very successful scheme, known as 'the yellow card scheme', is operated jointly by the Committee on Safety of Medicines (CSM) and the Medicines Control Agency. Information is provided by the prescriber on a yellow card, which is then submitted to the scheme. Copies of yellow cards can be found at the rear of the BNF, in MIMS and in the *Summary of Product Characteristics*. They can also be obtained by dialling 100 and asking for Freephone CSM or dialling 0800 731 6789 (see 'Adverse Reactions to Drugs' in BNF).

The function of the scheme incorporates the following objectives:

- to collect reports on any reactions to a new drug
- to gather serious reactions to established products even when the cause is not definitely established
- to maintain patient and professional confidence in prescribed drugs
- to provide early warnings of previously unsuspected adverse drug reactions
- to collate and compare adverse drug reactions between medicines within the same therapeutic class
- to look for factors that predispose to adverse reactions to specific drugs.

The reporting of adverse reactions has been limited to doctors, dentists, hospital and community pharmacists and Her Majesty's Coroners. Any nurse (not just nurse prescribers) who identifies, or is suspicious, that a patient has suffered an adverse reaction to a medicinal product, should encourage doctors or pharmacists to complete a yellow card and include the relevant doctor's name and address before submitting this to the CSM. It is thought that only about 10 per cent of serious and fatal reactions are ever reported (Pirmohamed et al. 1998). This might increase if additional health professionals were involved in reporting.

Quantities to prescribe

Quantities issued on prescription must be calculated in relation to expected 'normal' usage levels and the frequency with which the patient is seen.

Creams and ointments are often needed as emollients and soap substitutes for eczema and psoriasis sufferers. A common complaint from dermatologists and patients is that inadequate quantities of skin products are prescribed (Poyner 1996; Livingstone 1997). This results in poor compliance with therapy, flare-ups of skin conditions and probable increases in steroid usage. This is an example of short-sighted prescribing causing future and long-term problems.

Examples of realistic quantities of aqueous cream emollient for 1 month for an adult are:

- localised eczema on the arms only: 500 g
- generalised eczema over most of the body: 6 x 500 g.

As a soap substitute, additional amounts of emulsifying ointment of 500–1,000 g will be needed, taking into account the number of washing facilities around the house, work and so on.

When prescribing modern wound management products, normal changing frequencies should be considered, when selecting appropriate quantities to prescribe. For example, five hydrocolloid dressings should be adequate for one month unless the patient has multiple areas of treatment or the product is being changed too frequently, when alternative products may be more suitable. In the nurse prescribing pilot scheme, the practice with the greatest cost reduction for prescribing had reviewed and rationalised the prescribing of such products within a nursing home (*Drug and Therapeutics Bulletin* Seminar 1996). The cost–benefit study (DoH 1992), prior to the pilot nurse prescribing scheme, demonstrated that nurses used dressings and other items in a cost-effective manner. It is important that regular independent educational updates are available to maintain the knowledge base necessary to support this prescribing.

Similar considerations are important for catheter and stoma care products, which comprise a huge proportion of the country's prescribing budget, with a huge potential for waste if excessive prescribing occurs. Products have expiry dates, and prefilled catheters have shorter than average dates. Stockpiling must therefore be discouraged and quantities should be based on average usage, as detailed in the Drug Tariff. The following examples should raise awareness of issues to consider when asked to prescribe an item in this category:

1. Reusable Nelaton catheters for intermittent catheterisation come in packs of five. One catheter can be used for 5–7 days. One pack of five is therefore adequate for patients receiving monthly prescriptions. However, use of single-use catheters for intermittent self-catheterisation is increasing and as these are considerably more expensive, appropriate quantity selection is important, while minimising inconvenience to patients. These are in packs of 25 which cannot be split.

2. Drainable leg bags are available in packs of ten, which is more than enough for a monthly prescription, as these have a similar life to the reusable catheters. Packs may be split if necessary.

Product selection, communication and patient compliance

Product selection

In addition to the many clinical issues involved in product selection, the prescriber must also consider ease of use and patient acceptability, which will often relate to a patient's lifestyle. However, these considerations play only a part in achieving success with long-term therapy.

Collection of the prescription – why is this not 100 per cent?

A significant number of patients who are given a prescription in the UK never actually get it dispensed. The rate of this 'non-presentation' for GP-generated prescriptions is about 5 per cent but may be up to 20 per cent or more in elderly patients (Beardon et al. 1993). Since elderly people do not pay prescription charges, motivation rather than finance is the contributing factor. The figure relating to nurse-generated prescriptions is as yet unknown, but the comparison would be interesting. Prescribers must always remember that patients do not always feel that a prescription is appropriate for their needs.

Reasons are many and varied, but lack of satisfaction with the consultation, including inadequate explanation by the prescriber, plays a part. Good prescriber–patient communication is thus a vital part of the prescribing process to increase the likelihood of patient concordance with the chosen therapy.

Provision of patient information

The essential components of patient–prescriber discussion should include the following:

- the reason for the prescription
- the name and purpose of the medicine, including whether it will treat the condition, for example paracetamol for fever control, or just control symptoms, as do emollients in the management of eczema
- the length of treatment that will be needed both before an effect is seen and in total
- the significance of missed doses, and necessary action
- how to recognise adverse effects
- the concurrent use of over-the-counter and other medicines.

Basic information on the use of the product should never be overlooked even if patients have received the product before. An example is a patient on inhaler therapy, who may be found to have poor inhaler technique even though repeat prescriptions have been received for years.

Information on the use of nurse-prescribed items, together with GP-generated items, is also important. For example, the parent of a child with eczema may be unclear about the roles of the emollient prescribed by the nurse and the steroid cream provided by the GP or dermatologist and whether both can be applied together. Unfortunately 'seamless care', even between professionals within the same team, may falter, with resulting confusion for patients.

Labelling of medicines

The label on the medicine must now always be computer generated by pharmacists and will contain the following information:

- the name of the product, which will be generic for nurse prescriptions, except for the few exceptions highlighted in the NPF
- the name of the patient
- the date of dispensing
- the total quantity dispensed
- the directions for use
- the name and address of the supplying pharmacy
- advice to keep the medicine out of the reach of children.

Additional information that will be added by the pharmacist, for example 'take with or after food', 'dissolve in water' and so on, is indicated in the product monograph in the NPF.

Patients may ask for further explanation of these instructions and may quickly forget the additional verbal information provided by the pharmacist at the time of issue. They may then ask the next health professional with whom they have contact. As described earlier, nurse prescribers can obtain additional information on drug therapy from many sources, but the local community pharmacist should be a valuable resource. The pharmacist can also provide more user-friendly packs, when required, to help with specific problems, for example difficulty opening standard bottles.

For patients who are identified as poor compliers, the use of individual dosing systems (such as Nomad or Manrex) could be considered. However, if poor memory is the cause of poor concordance, these methods cannot guarantee success, although they may help to guide patients who are confused by the number of medications prescribed.

Oral syringes are routinely dispensed for the administration of liquid doses for volumes less than 5 ml. (This is of particular relevance to nurse prescribers when prescribing paracetamol for post-immunisation pyrexia.)

Repeat prescribing systems and the nurse prescribing process

All general practices should operate an efficient repeat prescribing policy. The aim of this should be to ensure that the ordering and provision of repeat prescriptions is safe and accurate, that there is an agreed 'normal' quantity issued (28 days, 30 days, and so on) and that patients are reviewed at an agreed frequency. This review should involve a consultation to establish the effectiveness of the medication, to monitor patients for side-effects and to confirm that there is a continuing need for the medication. All practice staff should work towards the safe operation of the system and should ensure that review dates are complied with and not over-ridden during busy times. If the review system is allowed to break down, patients rapidly fall into the habit of demanding repeats without ever seeing the original prescriber, and products are continued ad infinitum, with potentially disastrous results. It is stated in the *Nurse Prescribing Guidance* (NHS Executive HQ 1997) that 'the nurse should be mindful of any prescribing protocols agreed within the GP practice relevant to the patient' (p. 15). Practice protocols may need to identify items that are in the NPF but which nurses would not generally want to repeat without further consultation, for example clotrimazole cream.

The general guidance for repeat prescriptions (NHS Executive HQ 1997) is 'that no more than six repeat prescriptions should be made, or six months should elapse, whichever is the less, without re-assessing the patient's needs' (p. 14). The repeat system relies on the accurate entry of the initial prescription into the patient's medical records (often paper and computerised). Other prescribers in the practice may be asked to authorise future repeat prescriptions of items originally nurse prescribed. This is satisfactory provided that the original prescriber has indicated a review or reauthorisation date. The latter may be acceptable periodically for some patients and some products for which a regular chronic prescription is obtained, for example the emollients mentioned above for eczema. Such patients should still be reviewed to monitor them for infected eczema, to check progress of the eczema with the therapy provided and to give reassurance and answer the patient's questions. At two of the demonstration pilot sites for nurse prescribing, nurses conducted a review of repeat prescriptions, highlighting patients who were receiving repeat items that were in the NPF but that had originally been prescribed by doctors. At one of the sites, many products were found to be no longer required, and considerable savings were realised (Luker and Austin 1997). Following the second Crown Report (DoH 1999) it is likely that many more health professionals will be allowed to prescribe according to strict criteria as supplementary (dependent) prescribers, issuing repeat prescriptions and making dose adjustments. It is also very likely that allowable products will increase for certain specialist nurses and that the use of 'patient group directions' (formerly group protocols) will expand.

Lost prescriptions or requests for duplicate prescriptions

Requests for immediate repeat prescriptions or within a few hours or days of the original issue do occur, and a strict policy should be adopted. If, after questioning the patient, the request appears to be genuine ('The bottle broke!'), a further prescription could be given and the records clearly marked.

Disposal of unwanted medicines

All prescribers should encourage the safe disposal of unwanted medicines, whether discontinued and no longer needed, or having expired. Patients should be encouraged to return such items to community pharmacists. Most participate in an official scheme using safe 'dumping' containers that are collected from the pharmacy on a regular basis and incinerated. No medication, however small in size or volume, should be disposed of in domestic or commercial refuse, and disposal via the sewerage system is illegal, even for individuals, due to obvious potential dangers.

References

Barber, N. (1995) What constitutes good prescribing? *British Medical Journal*, **310**: 923–5.

Beardon, P.H.G., McGilchrist, M.M., McKendrick, A.D., McDevitt, D.G. and MacDonald, T.M. (1993) Primary non-compliance with prescribed medication in primary care. *British Medical Journal*, **307**: 846–8.

Current Problems in Pharmacovigilance CSM/MCA (2000) *Reminder: St John's Wort interaction*, **26**: 6–7.

DoH (1992) *Nurse Prescribing – a Cost Benefit Study*. DoH, London.

DoH (1999) *Review of Prescribing, Supply and Administration of Medicines. Final Report* (Crown II Report). DoH, London.

Drug and Therapeutics Bulletin Seminar (1996) Nurse prescribing issues. *Pharmaceutical Journal*, **257**: 764–5.

Health Service Circular (March 1999) *Clinical Governance: Quality in the New NHS*. NHS Executive HSC 1999/065.

Livingstone, C. (1997) Eczema. *The Pharmaceutical Journal*, **259**: 507–9.

Luker, K. and Austin, L. (1997) Nurse prescribing; study findings and GP views. *Prescriber*, **8**: 31–4.

NHS Executive HQ (1997). *Nurse Prescribing Guidance*, April. NHS Executive, Leeds.

Pirmohamed, M., Breckenridge, A.M., Kitteringham, N.R. and Kevin Parke, B. (1998) Adverse drug reactions. *British Medical Journal*, **316**: 1295–8.

Poyner, T. (1996) A rational approach to prescribing for eczema. *Prescriber*, **7**: 45.

Scally, G. and Donaldson, L. (1998) Clinical governance and the drive for quality improvement in the new NHS in England. *British Medical Journal*, **317**: 61–5.

6 The management of prescribing

Mark Campbell

This chapter describes some key aspects of the current framework within which primary care prescribing is both undertaken and managed, and places nurses' prescribing in context within this. A complex web of factors influences prescribing; there is therefore a wide range of management strategies. Some are determined nationally (for example, by the DoH or reflecting wider government policy), while others are locally driven at primary care trust (PCT)[1] level. This chapter considers mainly medicines prescribed in primary care rather than treatment in hospitals or self-treatment. The terms 'drug' and 'medicine' will be used interchangeably.

Background

Although many medicines are prescribed for symptom control in acute, self-limiting illnesses, the majority of use is probably for the treatment of common chronic diseases, for most of which drug treatment is a central feature. Prescribing therefore has a public health function – to lessen morbidity and (hopefully) reduce mortality. The pharmaceutical armamentarium increases by about 15 new drugs each year, while new clinical evidence continues to appear for existing drugs, making the choice of treatment increasingly difficult. Within this process, the NHS commits huge amounts of health care professional and patient time to prescribing. The cost of prescribing is also substantial; the GP drugs bill according to the PPA was, in 1999/2000, about £5.2 billion in England, accounting for about 15 per cent of total NHS expenditure and by far the largest proportion of NHS costs after staff. This amount represents about £90 per head of population per year. For most of the 1990s, primary care prescribing costs have risen on average by 8 per cent per annum, usually by at least three times the rate of increase in funding for the NHS as a whole. Promoting appropriate and effective prescribing while containing the rise in prescribing costs is therefore a considerable challenge.

Life cycle of prescription

After a prescription form (FP10 in England and Wales, GP10 in Scotland) is issued, it is dispensed either by a pharmacist, dispensing doctor or appliance contractor. The form is then sent to the Prescription Pricing Authority (PPA) for pricing and reimbursement of the drug costs and overheads to the dispensing contractor. The prescription data are also incorporated into a variety of electronic and hard copy prescribing information systems for feedback to prescribers (see below). At present, all prescriptions are issued as paper forms. In coming years, the proportion of prescriptions transmitted electronically between prescriber and dispenser will increase following pilot schemes during 2001. In addition, Internet-based pharmacy services will develop where 'prescriptions' are transmitted electronically to an online pharmacy which then delivers the medicines directly or by post.

Drug pricing

Branded drugs

Manufacturers' list prices – as shown in the *British National Formulary* (BNF) or the commercial *Monthly Index of Medical Specialities* (MIMS) – for branded drugs are set by means of a joint agreement between the DoH and individual pharmaceutical companies – the Pharmaceutical Price Regulation Scheme (PPRS). Within this scheme, a price is agreed for a new drug that represents between 17 and 25 per cent profit-on-return (POR). For existing medicines, companies must apply to the DoH to increase the price of the drug. If this is agreed, the POR must nevertheless remain within the target range. Increases in the price of existing drugs are unusual and there is usually little or no price inflation – but see the section below on generic medicine prices during 1999/2000.

Arguably, the PPRS maintains the price of branded drugs at artificially high levels, but this view overlooks the importance of the domestic pharmaceutical industry to the UK economy. For example, the pharmaceutical industry is the UK's second largest exporter by worth (in excess of £2 billion per annum) and a large provider of high-calibre employment. One undesirable consequence of the PPRS is that drugs with essentially similar therapeutic effects may vary considerably in price. For example, the world's biggest-selling pharmaceuticals, the anti-ulcer proton pump inhibitors such as omeprazole ('Losec') have no clinically important differences yet differ in price by up to 20 per cent.

The PPRS is renegotiated every five years; in 1993 and 1998, the renegotiations resulted in substantial drug price reductions resulting in real prescribing cost growth reductions of about 3 per cent (equivalent to £150 million) for the NHS.

Generic medicines

Until 2000, the supply and sale of generic medicines – unbranded drugs whose patent has expired – operated as a 'free market' with prices determined by conventional supply and demand principles. During 1999, a number of factors resulted in very large price increases in a wide range of commonly used generic drugs. For example, the price of low-dose aspirin for prevention of heart disease increased, at one point, to three times normal. The effects of this were severe financial pressure on primary care drug budgets and action by the DoH to regulate generic drug prices by imposing maximum prices for the drugs affected. Further changes are likely in the way that generic drugs are supplied and priced as a result of a long-term review by the DoH.

Discounts

In the UK, hospitals may buy some drugs at considerable discount on manufacturers' list prices. These discounts are not generally available in primary care, although, unlike for hospitals, VAT is not charged on drugs. Since the choice of drug in hospitals often influences prescribing in primary care, there is a potential problem when the drugs are bought at significant discount but whose high list prices are borne by primary care prescribers when asked to continue treatment.

Prescription charges

Although controversial, most countries with state-funded health care systems have some form of prescription tax or 'co-payment'. In the UK, this is a flat-rate levy, unrelated to the cost of the individual prescription drug. In some other countries, patients pay a proportion of the cost of the drug, usually up to a maximum payment. Increases in prescription charges are thought to have an impact on the number of prescriptions dispensed (but not necessarily the number issued), and there is concern that charges act as disincentive to have prescriptions dispensed. Nevertheless, prescription charges remain a significant source of revenue (about £300 million annually). There is a long-running debate over exemption from charges on the grounds of chronic illness, age or income (or whether there should be charges at all), and the current framework contains many inconsistencies. However, a better system has yet to emerge.

Selected list

Some countries operate mandatory or voluntary national formularies of 'preferred' drugs. In the UK, this policy has never gained much favour; instead, some drugs, usually on the basis of limited clinical value, are prohibited from FP10 prescription and other drugs in the same class promoted as alternatives. In 1985, the first selected list (then called a limited list) was published, in which some benzodiazepines, cough medicines and vitamin preparations became non-prescribable at NHS expense. The policy probably achieved some economies but was very unpopular among prescribers and patients. It has rarely operated since apart from topical non-steroidal anti-inflammatory drugs where a maximum treatment cost (or reference price) was set, based upon the lowest-price preparation available. Any preparation that costs more than this maximum would not be prescribable; all manufacturers subsequently adjusted the price of their products downwards to this level.

Financial incentives

Prior to 1991, there was no upper (or lower) limit on GP prescribing costs. However, the 1991 NHS White Paper introduced indicative prescribing amounts (IPAs), which were the best estimate of a practice's prescribing needs for a year. For practices that elected to be fundholders, the IPA became a real cash amount, and savings on the practice fund, of which the IPA was one element, could be retained and reinvested in improving local patient services. Subsequently, in 1993, this incentive was extended to non-fundholders. The impact of these schemes has been evaluated, and, although the picture is not clear cut, some important principles have emerged:

- Financial incentives are effective in improving budgetary discipline; fundholders consistently out-performed non-fundholders at budget adherence, although whether this is because they have received a disproportionately large budget share is unclear
- Fundholder and non-fundholder savings were generally made by simple means, such as increased generic prescribing
- The reductions in cost growth achieved by fundholders were not, overall, sustainable. In longer-term studies, cost growth among fundholders and non-fundholders was eventually similar.

Financial incentives are now an integral part of practice prescribing allocations; more recently, incentive schemes have included additional, locally determined, prescribing quality criteria.

One constant criticism of financial incentives is that they depend on the method used to determine the practice prescribing allocation. Originally, historical patterns of expenditure were used to determine practice budgets but, more recently, most practice allocations have been set with reference to an average local spend – the capitation benchmark. Practices with high baseline per capita costs receive a lower than average increase in allocation year-on-year and vice versa. Although imperfect, this system is an improvement on earlier methods. Practice allocations also take account of specific circumstances such as high-cost specialist drugs and residential and nursing home patients. The development of nurse prescribing presents additional difficulties in budget setting. First, no historic prescribing exists for comparison. Second, a local average cannot readily be calculated since community nurses do not, unlike GPs, have a registered patient list.

The formation of PCTs has had a major impact upon community nurse prescribing. PCTs, rather than community trusts, will employ – and be responsible for – nurse prescribing. In time, this will allow a more integrated approach to management of nurse prescribing and will make the financial framework easier to understand and manage since nurses' prescribing will be charged directly to practice budgets.

Prescribing information and feedback

Prior to 1988, there was little feedback to individual GPs on their own prescribing habits and no detailed information for the monitoring of prescribing at any level other than regional or national. The introduction of prescription analysis and cost (PACT) reports, which followed computerisation of the PPA, has allowed an increased awareness both of variations in prescribing and of trends. A wealth of prescription information is available at different levels of organisational detail (GP, practice, PCT, HA, regional and national) and drug detail (preparations, drugs, therapeutic areas and total prescribing) in different media to different users. GPs receive a paper summary report each quarter, whereas NHS organisations have electronic access at a level of detail appropriate to their needs.

Although comprehensive and understandable, PACT reports do not yet provide sufficient detail to understand fully the complexity of prescribing. In particular, the system is focused upon the drug prescribed; patient data (for example, age, sex and diagnosis) are not yet being collected. In order to overcome this, PACT data have been used to derive simple prescribing indicators that might, for example, be based on the choice of drugs in a therapeutic group or the level of prescribing of drugs where there is only limited evidence of efficacy. Work is ongoing to develop appropriate indicators for nurse prescribing.

A further problem that indirectly affects PACT is the increasing trend of buying medicines over the counter in pharmacies and of private prescriptions. Since these items are not routinely captured, PACT is incomplete as a global record of medicine utilisation.

Community nurses do not yet receive feedback on their prescribing directly from the PPA; instead, community trusts and PCTs have access to paper and electronic information on prescribing and have instituted local feedback and monitoring arrangements.

Evidence-based medicine, guidelines, protocols and formularies

The evaluation of available evidence in order to support prescribing decision-making is both difficult and time consuming. One of the most common ways of implementing evidence-based decisions is by means of written guidelines, protocols or drug formularies, in which treatments are recommended only if supported by good research evidence.

Such initiatives are usually local, at the level of a PCT or health authority, or sometimes within an individual GP practice. Hospitals have traditionally had local drug formularies and some GP practices have devised their own formularies. Although in theory an attractive way of making objective guidance available to a large audience, guidelines and protocols often fail to be successfully introduced and used.

Common problems include: they are not seen as locally relevant; end-users do not feel that they have 'ownership' of the guidelines; the guidelines are cumbersome to use, for example a bulky publication instead of a pocket-sized one. A particular problem can arise in some areas of nursing care when only limited or poor-quality research evidence is available. In such cases, guidelines based on the consensus opinion of 'national' experts may be received poorly by individual practitioners, each of whom perceives him- or herself to have at least as much expertise and/or experience.

Recently, the National Institute for Clinical Excellence (NICE) was formed to provide objective, evidence-based advice guidance to the NHS to achieve consistency in care and treatment. NICE publishes both appraisals of individual technologies and more generally applicable clinical guidelines. Its work programme includes several nursing topics, and guidelines on wound care and on pressure ulcer assessment and prevention were published in April 2001 (www.nice.org.uk).

Face-to-face contact

Management strategies for prescribing are implemented through HAs, PCTs and their professional prescribing advisers (usually doctors and pharmacists). These advisers are responsible for setting and monitoring prescribing allocations as well as promoting high-quality, cost-effective prescribing. Face-to-face contact is known to be the most effective behaviour change strategy, but the opportunity for this, with the average PCT having two to five advisers and up to 20 or more practices, is limited. Increasingly, other professionals, such as community pharmacists and specialist nurses, are being used to assist practices in changing their prescribing practice. Prescribing support teams are becoming increasingly involved in providing advice and support to community nurse prescribers.

Repeat prescribing

Since most medicines are used for chronic disease, they are given long term. This means that a high proportion of drugs are given as repeat prescriptions, so the organisation of practice systems for their issue is a potential source of improving long-term drug treatment and reducing inappropriate usage. Repeat prescriptions are usually defined as those for drugs that have already been initiated and subsequently repeated without a face-to-face consultation with a doctor. Although many patients on (often multiple) repeat prescriptions are not adequately reviewed, there is no universally agreed 'model' system for achieving this. Most initiatives to improve repeat prescribing have been locally driven and nurse prescribers will increasingly be involved in improving repeat prescribing.

Compliance and waste

Estimates of the rate of primary non-compliance (prescriptions being issued but not dispensed) are between 5 and 20 per cent. Even worse, when prescriptions have been dispensed, only half are taken as intended. The reasons for this are complex and outside the scope of this chapter, but non-compliance is a major concern for which the solutions are preventing inappropriate prescribing and providing better information for patients through counselling by health care professionals. Non-compliance also leads to waste; local DUMP (Disposal of Unwanted Medicines) campaigns collect tons of unwanted and unused drugs each year. Nurses working in the community are in a unique position to detect the 'hoarding' of medicines by patients and, at present, are probably underused in helping to address this problem.

Postgraduate education and training

There is a wide range of provision for postgraduate education, including that on therapeutics, for GPs in the UK, some of it arranged formally through regional postgraduate deans who are responsible for accrediting appropriate educational events under the Post Graduate Education Allowance scheme. This is a financial incentive for GPs to accrue a specified amount of approved educational time each year. However, the vast majority of the postgraduate education and training events on prescribing are sponsored by, and may be delivered by, the pharmaceutical industry. There is an obvious conflict of interest in such events although, in many cases, they are claimed to be organised on a non-promotional basis.

Nurse prescribers have substantial ongoing education and training needs on prescribing and therapeutics. No formal accreditation and funding schemes exist; instead, most post-qualifying education and training is organised through informal nurse prescribers' support groups. The National Prescribing Centre has provided a range of very useful publications and educational events for nurse prescribers.

The pharmaceutical industry

Overall, the pharmaceutical industry represents a very successful and profitable business. Its research and development activities have produced drugs that have reduced morbidity and mortality. It is also very skilful at promoting its products. It is prudent therefore to exercise a degree of caution in relationships between the NHS and the pharmaceutical industry. For example, claims made for new drugs or preparations often require further scrutiny; at the time of launch, the available evidence may, for example, be incomplete. All NHS staff, including nurses, have a duty to maintain high standards of professional business conduct and revised guidance on commercial sponsorship has recently been issued.

Patient group directions, supplementary prescribers, and extensions to nurse prescribing

The next few years will see further major changes in the supply, administration and prescribing of medicines by nurses, prompted in part by two major reviews on medicines led by Professor June Crown.

Patient group directions

The first Crown Report (DoH 1989) advocated that most treatment should continue to be prescribed on an individual basis but that more flexibility was needed in certain circumstances where a medical prescription was not available. One solution to this was a new initiative, the patient group direction (PGD, formerly called 'group protocol') a framework where, following a treatment protocol, health professionals other than doctors, could supply and/or administer medicines without a prescription. Although many thousands of PGDs have been developed, their importance will perhaps decline in the coming few years as more professionals are given prescribing powers.

Supplementary prescribers

The second Crown Report (DoH 1999) concluded that more groups of health professionals – including nurses, pharmacists and therapists – should be able to prescribe in their own right, either following carefully defined protocols (so called 'supplementary' prescribers) or independently as for doctors and dentists. The Health and Social Care Bill (2001) provided for the necessary legislation for these changes but full implementation is likely to take several years.

Extension to nurse prescribing

In the original nurse prescribing scheme, only nurses with – or studying towards – a district nurse or health visitor qualification were eligible to be trained and, once qualified, could only prescribe from a limited formulary. The DoH announced during 2001 that both the range of medicines prescribable and the number of prescribing nurses should be increased. For example, from May 2001, nurse prescribers may prescribe nicotine replacement therapy to help smokers quit while from 2002 a further 10,000 nurses will begin to be trained to prescribe a wide range of treatments, from an expanded NPF, for minor injuries such as burns, cuts and bruises; minor ailments such as hayfever and ear infections; health promotion such as pre-conceptual vitamins; and palliative care.

Note

1. Primary care organisations representing, on average, populations of about 100,000 people and which develop from primary care groups (PCGs). By 2002, almost all PCGs will have undergone the transition to primary care trust status and all will be responsible for improving the health of their population and commissioning local services.

Further reading

Consumers' Association/*Drug and Therapeutics Bulletin*/National Prescribing Centre. *Medicines and the NHS – a Guide for Directors.* Which Ltd, London.
http://www.which.net/health/dtb/mednhs.html.

References

DoH (1998) *Review of prescribing, supply and administration of medicines. A report on the supply and administration of medicines under group protocols.* DoH, London.
http://www.doh.gov.uk/pub/docs/doh/protocol.pdf.
DoH (1999) *Review of prescribing, supply and administration of medicines. Final report on the supply and administration of medicines under group protocols.* March 1999.
http://www.doh.gov.uk/pub/docs/doh/prescrib.pdf.

7

Keep taking your medication or you will not get better. Who is the non-compliant patient?

Joel Richman

The concept of the non-compliant patient is a product of what Foucault (1976) calls the 'medical gaze', a clinical construct embedded in its practical and ideological perspective which states that patients who do not follow doctors' orders must be deviants. Non-compliance covers a range of assumed patient behaviour: those who misuse prescribed medication, fail to change their lifestyles to alleviate illness, or neglect clinical attendance. We shall examine the medication aspect here, primarily based on research relating to doctors' consultations. It has obvious reference and significance for prescribing nurses, who must not automatically assume that all their patients will be happy to follow their instructions, because nurses might adhere more to a 'social model' of medicine.

The chapter will attempt to locate the social conditions conducive for non-compliance; this includes styles of consultation in general and psychiatric medicine. The next purpose is to outline the strategies used to produce patient conformity and to raise some of the ethical implications of these. Finally, the patient's view is posited, elaborating the complexities of lay reasoning about illness, in which its existential qualities linking to medication are mapped out. Illness is intimately wrapped round notions of the self, disturbing its favourable presentation. Medication is a symbolic and practical intrusion, often adding another conflicting dimension to the self's attempts not to be defined by illness per se.

A non-compliant patient becomes deviant because he or she has violated one of the cardinal principles of the Parsonian (1951) sick role. The patient is obliged not only to seek out medical assistance when ill, but also passively to accept doctors' instructions regarding the managing of the illness, especially concerning medication regimes. Another patient duty is not to linger in the sick role beyond the doctor's legitimate expectations. This deviance also includes 'overcompliance' – the taking of unnecessary medication. Those who are unemployed find comfort and respectable status in the sick role. Those who cannot accept that their condition is a result of normal ageing also 'overmedicate'. Combined with the ideology of the sick role is the Weberian Protestant ethic (Weber 1947): we live in an economic, cost-effective world. The non-compliant patient has also violated the expertise and labours of the medical practitioner. That is why 'overdosers' on prescribed and non-prescribed medication in A&E departments are often referred to as 'rubbish' cases, unnecessarily wasting the time of clinical staff who could be deployed better. Some (for example Britten 1994) prefer the term 'adherence' rather than 'compliance', indicating more the patients' choice in issues of medication. Within the context of nurse prescribing the term concordance has gained popularity (National Prescribing Centre 1999) whereby the prescribing decision is viewed as a shared contract between patient and prescriber. Here, we stick with compliance, the term more generally used, bearing in mind its ideological bias and that conformists and non-conformists do not constitute two polarised positions: a patient can be compliant with one medical regime but not another.

Consultation styles

Szasz and Hollender (1956) were among the first to recognise that the Parsonian ideal-type model of the doctor–patient relationship was not the only one. Each style had implications for patient compliance.

The authoritarian consultation projects the image that patients are clinically 'insignificant'; if patients do not accept the style, they should get another doctor, and patients talk when 'requested'. The doctor gives only that information which he or she thinks is relevant, and patients are not encouraged to question clinical data. The inherent antagonistic relationship resulting is not conducive to compliance.

The permissive style (verging on laissez-faire) also does not generate patient compliance. Doctors are always seeking to please the patient, leading to unstructured sessions that make it difficult for the patient to get comprehensive information and that submerge the treatment goal.

The psychotherapeutic style assumes that patients' fears about treatment and medication are not genuine everyday ones. Instead, clients' responses are interpreted in a therapeutic way. Patients' questions resisting prescribed medication are interpreted as the product of unconscious motives, for example as a resistance to a father figure. There is a valuable lesson for nurses about the above style: do not indulge in 'therapy talk' to confuse medication requirements.

The participatory style (Korsch 1969) produces high rates of compliance (as it does in experimental group dynamics). Here, doctors assume that patients have rights to question and complain. The medical regime is tailored to the patient's everyday routine in a way that is realistic. This style is sometimes welded on to doctor–patient contracts, emphasising mutual responsibilities. Patients are best able to evaluate the doctor's human relations skills rather than technical ones. Bond and Salinger (1979) have shown that joint prescribing with psychiatrist and pharmacist for those with schizophrenia produces a higher rate of compliance. Patients' complaints are not treated as delusions or signs of denial but as real problems. Drug dosages are rapidly modified to cause fewer side-effects, especially posture and movement disorder effects. Poor control of the side-effects of psychotropic drugs is a major reason for non-compliance.

Evidence of non-compliance

There is no simple and uniform way of measuring non-compliance. Counting the pills left in a container and measuring the medicine level in a bottle both suffer from obvious defects. Stichele (1991, p. 30) argues that:

> Pill count grossly overestimates compliance, and misses some 10 per cent of overt non-compliers. False positive assessment of compliance occurs when patients deliberately discard tablets, before returning containers. This is called 'pill dumping' or the 'parking lot' phenomenon.

Therapeutic drug monitoring using venous blood samples is a cumbersome method of assessing compliance. For a few drugs, due to individual differences in pharmacokinetics, it can give misleading results. For example, with repeated dosing over a few weeks, the rate of clearance of chlorpromazine (and its active metabolites) may increase: this decreases the concentration of chlorpromazine in plasma. The low concentrations of chlorpromazine may be misinterpreted as evidence of non-compliance. The measurement of metabolite level is also not always a predictor: for example, those with bipolar affective disorder (manic depression) are stabilised on lithium carbonate, but the latter's absorption rate is extremely high. Drug testing in prisons has similar problems: heroin leaves little trace after 30 hours; marijuana, in contrast, is detectable up to 30 days after first taking it. Patient interviews are also notoriously unreliable. A founding father of ancient Greek medicine, Hippocrates, warned of patients' lies over 2,500 years ago. Mothers will lie on behalf of sick children lest they are not considered 'good mothers'. Sheiner et al. (1974) have demonstrated that doctors very frequently over-estimate the compliance levels of their own patients as a psychological boost to their own prestige. There are lessons here for the new, prescribing nurses, wanting medical acclaim for their skills.

A recent method for evaluating compliance is the addition to the prescribed medication of another low-dose substance as a pharmacological marker, one which is easily detected in blood or urine samples. Low dosages of digoxin were used in Finnish heart studies as part of the Karelia public health programme in the 1980s. In most Western developed nations, patients must consent to the use of pharmacological markers because, strictly speaking, they are not integral to the medication regime. Other pharmacological markers have been suggested: radioactive substances; inert molecules, for example perfluorocarbon; stable isotopes, for example C-glucose or C-benzoid acid; and low-dose phenobarbitone of 2 mg/day, used because of its half-life of four days in adults. Patients are generally more conformist when they are informed that they are going to have, for example, a blood or urine test as part of their care plan. Without pharmacological markers, blood levels per se are very inaccurate: the latter is affected by lean body mass: fat ratios, gastric acidity levels and so on (Freely and Cooke 1987). A new generation of electronic monitoring devices is coming on the market, for example aerosol sprays that activate external, graduated scales (very much on the same principle as longlife batteries, allowing the user to know how much power is left). In spite of the extra expense, it is still not possible to say that the user has used the spray effectively for his or her particular condition. When counselling is built into treatment regimes, patients become more 'honest' about their compliance rates, as indicated in hypertension studies in the USA (Levine 1979).

Some features of non-compliance

Studies of non-compliance indicate the following:

- Anyone can be a non-compliant patient. Doctors themselves are notorious for being non-compliant when ill.
- The number of articles on non-compliance has been doubling every five years, indicating how seriously the medical profession regards the theme.
- The proportion of patients who fail to comply fully with prescribed treatment is around 30–60 per cent. With some medicines, this can be as high as 90 per cent.
- When patients fail to improve on medication, doctors tend to resort to blaming the patient (victim) for not taking the medication correctly. Carmeli's (1976) study of doctor–patient relationships in a diabetic clinic demonstrated that doctors' diagnostic reasoning was akin to that of magic used in tribal society. It was a ritualised, closed system of thought excluding the scientific possibility that, for example, the batch of insulin used by patients was faulty. Instead, the patient was regarded as the cause of the 'malevolence' regarding the fluctuation of glucose level displayed. The newly introduced human insulin was automatically assumed by the medical establishment to be better than the long-used insulin derived from pigs. Again, patients' complaints about it were dismissed as 'not possible' for the new insulin matched better the human condition. Later research showed that patients' doubts were correct: the human insulin gave less body warning about sinking into hypogly-caemic attacks.

- Non-compliance is far more than misunderstanding (bad communication) between doctor and patient, although Ley et al. (1976) have shown that, on leaving clinics and surgeries, patients forget 37–54 per cent of information that they have been given.

- Non-compliance is not related solely to social class, marital status, age or IQ: even children can cheat. Belmonte (1981) showed how diabetic children cheated when taken away to summer camp. It was assumed that the children would be more conformist to the strict, diabetic, self-administered regimen in groups, which would establish conformist norms of behaviour. Instead, children falsified their sugar level readings, believing, logically, that if their level were 'low', they were recovering. Many adults also have a 'make-believe' attitude to their own illness, 'willing it to their order'.

- Non-compliance is more likely to be a 'problem' (a) if drugs are taken over a long period of time, and (b) the more drugs are prescribed, with varying frequency of ingestion (Conrad 1985).

- Compliance is poor if medication is expensive. (This does not apply primarily to the UK.) This is especially true in less-developed nations: the poor, who have to pay a considerable part of their meagre income on drugs, will tend to dilute medication to make it 'last longer'. Many of the medicines for sale could also be out of date (Taylor 1986). The same behaviour occurs with poor blacks in the USA ghettos: they will frequently not take prescriptions to be dispensed. It should be noted that approximately 40 million Americans have no health insurance.

- There is a much higher level of compliance if the disease (for example, some sexually transmitted diseases like gonorrhoea) is short term, symptomatic, painful and publicly distressing.

- Compliance is poor if 'side-effects' are severe. In fact, there is no such thing as a 'side-effect', only the effects of the drugs. Some drugs for hypertension are known to make the patient feel worse; 40 per cent of the USA population has high blood pressure, unbeknown to them, and hypertension, if untreated, is a 'silent killer'. What can be listed as severe side-effects varies according to personal judgement. Some patients stop taking chlorpromazine for schizophrenia because they put on weight. In fact, the drug does not cause weight increase but makes patients very thirsty, many then drinking heavily sugared soft drinks. There are also other factors involved: Chlorpromazine increases appetite, due to alpha and dopamine blockade in the hypothalamus. This latter effect is a latent aspect of the medication. Psychiatric nurses locked into the medical model of care very often become concerned only about the frequency of dosage, neglecting social drinking habits.

• Those at the extremes of age tend to be among the most non-compliant. Those over 75 years are the major consumers of medicine because of their increasing chronicity. However, their diminishing mental and visual competence makes it difficult for many to read, follow prescribing instructions and discriminate the colours of pills. In 2001, there will be one million people aged over 85 years in the UK, three-quarters of whom will be women; most of this age group will live alone. About 25 per cent will develop Alzheimer's disease and other severe dementias. Many will also be physically unable to open child-proof medication containers. Physical and cognitive impairment is not the only factor behind aged non-compliance. Many have, during their life-time, experienced the fad of new 'miracle drugs' and hence are sceptical of the hyped claims being made for recent drugs. Some, not only the aged, develop the fear of becoming 'addicted' to their medication or of its poisoning them. Donovan and Blake (1992) reported that about 20 per cent of their sample of rheumatology patients gave the fear of 'addiction' as a reason for their non-compliance. The increased media attention on addiction to medications for depression by women prescribed Ativan has created moral panics wider than the drug focused upon. There is also a parallel with the scare stories about oral contraceptives, although the medical risks associated with these are very small.

• Compliance is very high in situations where people have life-threatening diseases and are offered experimental treatment as the only hope. Fox (1959) described a metabolic ward where patients became 'quasi-colleagues' to their doctors. The latter gave patients maximum information, as they wanted them to be reliable monitors of the effects of the new drug. Doctors very often named their patients in resulting publications, thanking them for enduring so much discomfort for the sake of the experiments.

- Patients' knowledge of disease and treatment is not always conducive to medication conformity. Dialysis patients are very knowledgeable but are often non-compliant, especially immediately before commencing dialysis treatment on machines and as teenagers. The one aspect they most conform to is that of the phosphate-binding medicine (for preventing heart attacks). There is little association between supportive family networks and compliance (yet network support was often a criterion for 'rationing' dialysis when the technique was in its infancy). The supportive network will support the patient no matter what the dialysand does. However, the degree to which the patient regards his or her behaviour as being disruptive of family life in general is more related to compliance (Cummings 1982).

Ethnicity and compliance

As yet, very little research has been done illustrating compliance in different ethnic groups. One of the relevant issues is that many from multicultural backgrounds have lay beliefs of health different from the assumptions of the Western bioscientific model. For example, many Afro-Caribbeans have an externalising health belief system (Table 7.1). That is, their notion of medical causation lies outside the body, often being of a personalistic nature. This, as Richman (1987, p. 12) says:

> explains disease etiology by the 'purposeful' interventions of agents deliberately pursuing their victims, causing them to fall ill. The malevolence can be human [witches], non-human [ancestors and other spirits] or 'supernatural' [deities].

The belief is that, by breaking some values of moral order, the external causation of illness will then target them. They also believe that others can target misfortune on them. The body in an externalising belief system is therefore a receptacle for the illness. In Western society, the body is mainly the source of illness pathology. The bioscientific model has an internalising health belief system (Table 7.1), often 'fighting' illness by developing a new chemical drug level producing a body equilibrium. It is relevant to point out that most UK natives also have an externalising lay belief model of illness causation. I have frequently heard from

Table 7.1 Health beliefs

	Internalising	Externalising
1. Source of illness	Within the body, for example a virus	Outside the body, for example tension in relationships breaking moral codes
2. Causation	Multiple	Fewer, for example the same cause having multiple disease effects
3. Proof of improvement	Empirical scientific	Symbolic
4. Body	Complex physical	Simple; for example the body differentiation is often a 'black box' and a receptacle for disease
5. Practitioner	Treats the individual client; passivity	Treats the individual as part of sets of expected relationships to reconcile disharmony
6. Health knowledge	Monopoly of specialists	Widely dispersed in society, which gives clients great 'pull' on healers
7. Society	Complex division of labour, producing economic surpluses that support the élite	Simple division of labour, little surplus, very small 'leisured' élite or literati
8. Recovery from illness	When fit for work	When restored to the moral order of the group. For example the Cheyenne have a 7-day singing ceremony for the ill, each verse historically recreating the universe; then the sick person is finally incorporated into it

people with depression that the source of their complaint is partly retribution, and that depression, like a huge mist, wrapped itself around them so that they became lost.

Thus, in an internalising psychiatric setting, an Afro-Caribbean will get irritated by the psychiatrist's Sherlock Holmes style of diagnosis. Give her the clues (symptoms) and she will make the diagnosis. Afro-Caribbeans have another purpose. They know the causation of their illness, very often attributed to Obeah, a 'malevolent spirit', who has poisoned them, but they want the psychiatrist to tell them who has been responsible for directing Obeah towards them. The great limitation of the bioscientific model is that it is not in business to answer the questions frequently asked by all patients, for example 'Why has cancer attacked me'. The 'Why me?' stance questions one of the reasons for the 'overdiagnosis' of Afro-Caribbeans (especially male) with schizophrenia. When they talk of poisoning in the consultation, this is immediately latched on to by the psychiatrist as a symptom of the illness – penetration of the body boundary is a Rank Schneider symptom of schizophrenia. Thus those with external-ising health beliefs cannot conceptualise that Western, prescribed medication can cure them. They want the doctor to defend them against the outside evil force; they cannot conceptualise how a small pill will do that.

Strategies for compliance

Many strategies have been devised to overcome non-compliance:

- The use of fixed ratio combinations of medication, especially pills, simplifying the usual counting of mixed quantities of pills.
- Patient package inserts (PPIs) of 'full' information by the phar-maceutical company, including details of clinical trials and adverse effects ratios, slotted into the packaging. Again, it was assumed that better informed patients are compliant. Pressure from the American Medical Association had PPIs discontinued on the grounds that they were 'disrupting doctor–patient relations', that is, patients became more questioning of doctors' prescribing. Modified PPIs are used in UK packaging.
- Written contracts with patients setting out joint responsibil-ities. These originated in the USA, where discontented patients more often sue their practitioners.
- Counselling: This has been a difficult variable to evaluate, because there are so many different types of counselling, provided by different sources. That carried out by prescribing nurses in a clinic or home is different from that of a specialist therapist. Colcher and Bass (1972) showed that counselling

parents on the use of penicillin given to their children resulted in 20 per cent more adherence than occurred in those who were not counselled.

• Coercion, or forced medication, introduced by public pressure after some mentally ill patients killed after stopping medication. Supervised discharge (s. 23 of the Mental Health Act 1983) was introduced in April 1996. The patient's recognised medical officer has the power to place patients under supervised discharge if it is likely that they are a substantial risk to their own and others' safety. Patients can be required to attend hospital for medication. Psychiatric nurses also have the right to 'take and convey' patients to such places. Supervision registers are held by individual trusts at local level. The facts are that psychiatric patients discharged into the community have murdered at the rate of 18 persons, usually family members, per year; the overall murder rate is about 800 persons for annum, most being carried out by those without a mental disorder. It is obvious that compulsory medication can split a professional–patient relationship based on trust.

• Financial incentives for compliance are on the agenda. In the 1970s, Austria used them as a device for mothers' compliance with antenatal sessions; the infant mortality rate fell nationally as a result. France, with its diminishing population, has, since 1945, used attendance payments. Giuffrida and Torgerson (1997) have reviewed the financial schemes:

The incentives ranged from relatively small amounts of money ($5) up to gifts of nearly $1,000 for a treatment programme for cocaine dependency.

(p. 705)

Other schemes, all in the USA, have been for antituberculosis regimes (TB is increasing, with the rise in the number of homeless, and so on), to promote antihypertensive treatment, for weight-reducing programmes and for paediatric outpatient attendance. Ethical issues emerge with the use of financial incentives: how much is to come out of health budgets for them? Which conditions should be supported? Is cost-effectiveness to be the only consideration? For example, homeless people with TB can quickly spread it to the host population.

Subjects' rationale for non-compliance

Non-compliant patients can have sophisticated belief systems structuring their behaviour. Conrad's (1985) study of epileptics is an illustration of this. Patients frequently know that doctors have had difficulty in matching medication levels to their condition. Self-regulation is thus an attempt to round off the doctor's incomplete knowledge, to normalise themselves. Self-regulation mimics the doctor's prescribing fiat of 'try it and see' but is more finely tuned to individual needs. Self-regulation attempts to bring a sense of order to the body with its illness, which can appear hostile, uncontrollable and rebellious – all features undermining the self. The bioscientific model often treats illness as a thing, a reification separate from sensate experience, hence the doctor's oft-repeated gambit to the patient, 'What is it that brings you here today', as an opening greeting.

Conclusion

We have stressed that non-compliance is an ideological feature of the medical model, which has to compete with other worlds in which the patient engages – sex, leisure, work, family and so on. That is why it is impossible to produce the identity profile of the non-compliant patient. Whether the prescribing nurse will have extra time to explore patients' other worlds which link with medication remains to be seen: the average GP consultation lasts about 6 minutes. We must also not forget the overcompliant patient. Hulka et al. (1975) discovered that doctors were not aware of 19 per cent of medications that patients were taking. This is an issue with ethnic minorities who use, for example, both traditional healers (hakims) and the GP for the same complaint. Let Hulka close for us:

> The problem of non-compliance will remain with us, it is, after all part of the human condition. It will not be, and probably should not be, conquered altogether. Because many prescribed medications are not powerful over and above their placebo effects, non-compliance often does no harm. When patients refuse to do what physicians advise, as expressions of their own informed free will, it is also unclear that harm has been done.
>
> (p. 858)

Postscript

This addendum makes more explicit the power dimension within health occupations and society at large, impinging on the complex relationship subsumed under the simple category of 'non-compliance'. McCartney et al. (1999) frame the occupational power dimension in terms of their article, 'Nurse prescribing: radicalism or tokenism?' They inject a note of scepticism into the motives for the creation of the Medicinal Products: Prescription by Nurses Act 1992.

The 'deregulation' impetus of medicine by nurse prescribing allowing greater access to medicines and consumer choice was governed more by the desire to economise (value for money initiative) and to challenge the long entrenched hegemony of medicine rather than raise the status of nurses per se to that of doctors. The same can be said for the initiative allowing some higher grade nurses taking over some of the work done by junior doctors, whose hours have to be reduced by EC directives. Touche-Ross (DoH/Touche-Ross 1991), empowered to monitor nurse prescribing, have argued that the benefit of nurse prescribing outweighs its costs. Since most of the substances nurses prescribe to date are available over the counter the obvious question arises: Why are nurses' powers so limited? McCartney et al. (1999) come to the conclusion that nurse prescribing is a shot across the medical bow, first by the Conservatives then New Labour, indicating that unless medicine becomes less critical of governmental changes for the NHS the government will sponsor more nurse power within the primary health care groups/trusts. The introduction of the nurse consultant is a similar threat to doctors.

The macro power relations to be incorporated into the nurse prescribing/compliance debate concern the future of society. Here we have many new labels; for example post-industrialism, post Fordism, the information society, late Capitalism and so on. Giddens (1991, p. 5) argues convincingly that we have moved to a context of 'high modernity', accompanied by the 'dialectical interplay of the local and the global, the more individuals are forced to negotiate life style choices among a diversity of options'. He stresses that high modernity is a risk culture. Giddens does not mean that social life is riskier than before, but the 'concept of risk becomes more fundamental to the way lay actors and technical specialists organise the social world' (p. 3). For lay actors one can read non-compliant patients who experiment with their medication to fit their personal lifestyles. Non-compliant patients will perform their own version of risk assessment with their prescribed medications. In Giddens's words: 'self identity becomes a *reflexively* organised endeavour' (p. 5). The patient as self continuously refines his/her biography through the choices offered by a society of high modernity.

Globalisation and the future of medical compliance

High modernity is rapidly precipitating globalisation. For some this will mean exclusion; for others differentiation. Specifically for the compliance debates Giddens (1991, p. 9) comments:

> the body is less and less intrinsic, and 'given', functioning outside the internally referential systems of modernity (for example accepting doctors' orders) but becomes itself reflexively mobilised.

The body is now offered choices as in biological reproduction, cosmetic surgery and sexuality. People will seek out 'authenticity' as a dominant value. Hence it is predicted that more will be non-compliant/deviant (from the medical perspective) in the search for the 'real' self, which can be stunted by medication, especially that devised for mental illness, particularly schizophrenia. The government, worried by the trend resulting in some notorious killings, has produced an at risk register; psychiatric patients in the community can now be removed for compulsory medication, if they default and become a danger to themselves and others, because they have attempted to 'reclaim' themselves from clinical prescribing.

As Lee (2000, p. 6) remarks:

> globalisation is a term which has been used frequently in recent times to describe a wider range of processes in the health field. As a convenient catch all it has been cited as both cause and effect of many things.

It is not the purpose here to spell out all the ramifications: does it mean Americanisation, more inequalities in national power, more corporate influence, and so on? One general agreement is that globalisation means changes in the spatial–temporal dimension. Robertson (1992) argues that we sense the world as a single place: with advances in information technology we now live in a global village in the instant present. Cyberspace is our new community. The global culture of the Internet alters our cognitive dimension; we can now understand ourselves as global citizens sharing interests across national/cultural divides. New advances in scientific, medical discourses are accessible to all.

The Internet will have the following impact on doctor and nurse prescribing:

- Patients will be better informed about their illness and range of treatments
- Practitioners will be put under pressure to familiarise themselves with the mushrooming number of medical web sites
- Practitioners will have to give more details about a patient's illness, range of treatments and 'precise' effects of medication; the latter is not always possible
- Patients will double-check a clinician's diagnosis and so on and be more disputatious
- Some knowledgeable patients will want to be treated as colleagues and not patients, necessitating a wider range of consulting styles.

Some web sites are mainly for professionals and provide an online diagnostic service (for example www.medical-library.org – £6.25 for a year's subscription). NHS Direct (www.nhsdirect.uk) takes patients through a series of yes/no answers. For something serious you are told to ring NHS Direct or see your GP. Some GPs are refusing to publicise NHS Direct because it is sending too many 'minor aliments' to them. Patients can also email *Watchdog*'s Dr Mark Porter for replies. Another site gives a seven-minute check up (www.healthscout.com). Some sites also prescribe drugs (www.thedoctoronline.com) for which you pay £37. The *Manchester Evening News* (30 March 2000) dedicated a whole page to Sue Stacey, who had never used the Internet before but discovered that her kidney stones were actually cystinuria and that her healthy diet of fish and low fat meats, including turkey, had to be discarded because they exacerbate her condition. From the web site (www.cystinuria.com) she also discovered that one third of her watered intake should be consumed at night: cysteine builds up when lying down.

Finally, two future aspects of prescribing have been held up for inspection. First, that nurse prescribing is in its infancy. It is likely that the government will enlarge this if it is cost efficient; initial trials show this to be so. Nurse prescribing will be just one prong to cut into the medical hegemony. Second, globalisation has the potentiality to make patients (at least Western) more know-ledgeable, requiring a 'colleagueship' style of consultation and prescribing. The more rapid spread of the medical model into the developing world is also likely to undermine traditional healing patterns, a subject beyond the scope of this chapter. The exag-gerated status value placed on expensive vitamin/food supple-ments is partly responsible for the reduction in breastfeeding with its wider benefits. The pharmaceutical companies heavily advertise their products. They encourage the poor to spend a great deal of the household budget, for example on formula milk. When this is mixed with polluted water disease is easily transmitted to babies. Breastfeeding, which is safe, is portrayed by advertising as being primitive. The multinational Nestlé has been indicted for this bad practice and has modified some of its marketing strategies in the less developed world.

In conclusion, non-compliance by its universality should be regarded as a Durkheimian 'social fact', with multifarious modes. The doctor diagnoses for the 'generalised patient', the patient completes the diagnosis by particularising the process to accom-modate notions of the self.

References

Belmonte, T. (1981) Problem of cheating in diabetic child and adoles-cent. *Diabetic Care*, 7: 11–19.

Bond, C.A. and Salinger, P. (1979) Fluphenazine outpatient clinics, a pharmacist's role. *Journal of Clinical Psychiatry*, 22: 501–3.

Britten, N. (1994) Patients' ideas about medicines: a qualitative study in a general practice population. *British Journal of General Practitioners*, 44: 465–8.

Carmeli, T. (1976) Magical elements in orthodox medicine: diabetes as a medical thought system. Paper presented to the British Medical Sociological conference at York.

Colcher, I.S. and Bass, J.W. (1972) Penicillin treatment of streptococcal pharyngitis. A comparison of schedules and the role of specific counselling. *Journal of the American Medical Association,* **222**: 657–70.

Conrad, P. (1985) The meaning of medications: another look at compliance. *Social Science and Medicine,* **20**: 29–37.

Cummings, K.M. (1982) Psychosocial features affecting adherence to medical regimes in a group of haemodialysis patients. *Medical Care,* **10**: 567–95.

DoH/Touche-Ross (1991) *Nurse Prescribing – Final Report: a Cost Benefit Study.* Department of Health and Touche-Ross, London.

Donovan, J.L. and Blake, D.R. (1992) Patient non-compliance: deviance or reasoned decision making? *Social Science and Medicine,* **34**: 507–13.

Foucault, M. (1976) *The Birth of the Clinic.* Tavistock, London.

Fox, R. (1959) *Experiment Perilous.* Free Press, Glencoe, IL.

Freely, N. and Cooke, J. (1987) Low dose phenobarbitones as an indictor of compliance with drug therapy. *British Journal of Clinical Pharmacology,* **24**: 77–83.

Giddens, A. (1991) *Modernity and Self Identity: Self and Society in the Late Modern Age.* Polity Press, Cambridge.

Giuffrida, A. and Torgerson, D.J. (1997) Should we pay the patient? Review of financial incentives to enhance patient compliance. *British Medical Journal,* **315**: 703–7.

Hulka, B.S., Cassel, J.C., Gupper, L.L. and Efird, R.L. (1975) Communication, compliance and concordance between physician outpatients with prescribed medications. *American Journal of Public Health,* **66**: 847–58.

Korsch, S. (1969) Gaps in doctor patient communication. *New England Journal of Medicine,* **76**: 42–51.

Lee, K (2000) The global dimensions of health. In Parsons, L. and Lister, G. (eds) *Global Health: A Local Dimension.* The Nuffield Trust, London, pp. 6–16.

Levine, E. (1979) Health education for hypertensive patients. *Journal of American Medical Association,* **217**: 1700–3.

Ley, P., Bradshaw, D.W., Kincey, J.A. and Atherton, T.S. (1976) Increasing patient satisfaction with communication. *British Journal of Social and Clinical Psychology,* **15**: 403–13.

McCartney, W., Tyrer, S., Brazier, M. and Prayle, D. (1999) Nurse prescribing: radicalism or tokenism? *Journal of Advanced Nursing,* **20**: 348–54.

National Prescribing Centre (1999) Signposts for prescribing nurses – general principles of good prescribing. *Prescribing Nurse Bulletin,* **1**(1): 1–4.

Parsons, T. (1951) *The Social System.* Free Press, Glencoe, IL.

Richman, J. (1987) *Medicine and Health.* Longman, Harlow.

Robertson, R. (1992) *Globalization: Social Theory and Global Culture.* Sage, London.

Sheiner, L.B., Rosenberg, B., Marathe, V.V. and Peck, C. (1974) Differences in serum digoxin concentrations between outpatients and inpatients: an effect of compliance? *Clinical Pharmacological Therapy,* **15**: 239–46.

Stichele, R.V. (1991) Measurement of patient compliance and the interpretation of randomized clinical trials. *European Journal of Clinical Pharmacology,* **41**: 27–35.

Szasz, T.T. and Hollender, M.H. (1956) Contributions to the philosophy of medicine. The basic models of the doctor–patient relationship. *Archives of Internal Medicine,* **97**: 585–92.

Taylor, P. (1986) The pharmaceutical industry in the Third World. *Social Science and Medicine,* **22**: 1141–9.

Weber, M. (1947) *The Theory of Social and Economic Organisation.* Free Press, New York.

8 Nurse prescribing: the reality

Lorraine Lowe and Rita Hurst

Following the recommendations in the Crown Report (DoH 1989), nurse prescribing became a reality in 1994, involving eight pilot sites throughout the country. The literature charts the success of nurse prescribing for all those involved (Luker et al. 1997; Winstanley 1998). As part of one of the first eight national pilot sites for nurse prescribing we were both delighted and anxious to become prescribers. We agreed with the sentiments of Carlisle (1989) that the practice of the doctor having to 'rubber stamp' a prescribing decision taken by a nurse was demeaning to both nurse and doctor; in addition we found that this process wasted a considerable amount of time.

In reviewing a seven-year period of nurse prescribing while updating this chapter, we found that the prescribing practices for district nurses and health visitors have not substantially altered. However, one of the major shortcomings of nurse prescribing has been that it involves only a minority of community nurses. The publication of the *Review of Prescribing Supply and Administration of Medicines* (colloquially known as Crown II) in 1999 (DoH 1999) offers the potential for a range of health professionals to become prescribers, and the consultation on proposals to extend nurse prescribing (DoH 2000) considers which other nurses should prescribe. This chapter explores the role of the 'new' nurse prescriber, incorporating our own feelings when we were first in that position. We have also presented a picture of our own development in prescribing including case study scenarios and discussion of the benefits we found appertaining to nurse prescribing.

Dr Saul and Partners were chosen as one of the eight national pilot sites for nurse prescribing in May 1994. The commitment to the cause of nurse prescribing and the willingness to participate in data collection and evaluation at all stages were essential criteria for selection for the pilot sites (DoH 1989). Together with a practice nurse and another district nurse we were the four nurses who would become the first nurse prescribers in the northwest of England and be among the pioneers of nurse prescribing in the UK. When the eight pilot sites were announced, we were unprepared for the amount of media attention that became focused upon us as a team. Suddenly, we were being asked to give interviews for the radio, local newspapers and nursing publications. After the initial excitement and the surge of publicity, we had to prepare for the training course. It was at this stage that the reality set in and the real anxieties began to emerge. Although we knew that the nursing profession would be closely monitoring prescribing practices, we did not initially appreciate the impact that being part of the pilot would have on us personally. We had a limited time to complete the open learning component before the two-day course, and there was certainly a sense of panic when we were about to take the written examination. With the eyes of the country upon us, the fear of failure was very worrying. On reflection, although the course seemed rushed, the content was adequate for the *Formulary* as it was at that time. We could anticipate the potential benefits of prescribing, for both patients and professionals. Having waited eight years for nurse prescribing to become a reality, the four of us in Bolton were determined to make it viable.

The *Nurse Prescribers' Formulary*

The NPF was not allocated to us until the day we actually started prescribing (3 October 1994); however, the recommendation in the Crown Report (DoH 1989) gave some insight into its content. To some community nurses, the NPF seemed very limiting (see Appendix 1) and would possibly not provide enough scope to have any great impact on the delivery of patient care. However, over the 12-month pilot project, it was not just the actual content of what we were able to prescribe, nor the newly acquired prescribing status we had attained, but the enhanced approach to patient care that offered the most potential.

The NPF seemed to benefit the district nurses more than health visitors or practice nurses. The majority of the day-to-day items used by district nurses are in the *Formulary*. Products for wound care, catheter care and bowel management, all areas that are generally managed by district nurses, were covered by the NPF. For the health visitors and practice nurses, the NPF was more limiting.

During the pilot study, we were asked to identify products that we thought should be included in the *Formulary*, for example saline nasal drops, a wider variety of barrier preparations and emollients, eye drops, infant colic drops, soya products and topical antibacterial preparations. As a result of the evaluation study of the eight pilot sites, Luker et al. (1997) recommended that consideration should be given to the range of preparations for inclusion in the new NPF. It was recognised that the original NPF might be restricting practice and further evaluation was required in order to allow nurses to achieve greater autonomy and, as a result, to enhance patient care delivery. The 1999–2001 NPF added a few products although the original 12 chapters from the BNF remained unchanged. The latest information from the DoH (2001) is that independent nurse prescribers will soon be able to prescribe all general sales list and pharmacy medicines which are prescribable by doctors under the NHS.

Accountability and responsibility

When we qualified as prescribers, we recognised that this new role added another facet to our accountabilities. As nurses we recognise that we are accountable for our actions or omissions as stated in the UKCC *Code of Professional Conduct* (1992). Undertaking any role that has been traditionally the domain of the medical profession does not preclude nurses from taking responsibility for their actions.

We realised that the legal implications of nurse prescribing meant that, in a court of law, our actions would be compared against those of a reasonable doctor rather than a reasonable nurse (Tingle 1990). Hunt (1988) notes that, if a doctor can be sued for failing to warn about risks, equally a nurse can if he or she assumes the doctor's role. As new nurse prescribers, we felt quite anxious about the extra responsibility and accountability that signing prescriptions would place on us. Accountability not only means having to answer for an action when something goes wrong, but is also a continuous process of monitoring how we perform professionally (Tschudin 1986). We have been able to overcome some of our anxieties through peer group review and clinical supervision. Pearson (1987) defined peer review as:

> A process used to appraise the quality of a nurse's professional performance and is conducted by a group of nurses who are actively engaged in some component of practice.

During the peer review sessions, while maintaining patient confidentiality, we discussed patient case studies and the issues of prescribing. These sessions offered us the opportunity to discuss each other's roles and clarify responsibilities; in turn, the working relationships and communication within the primary health care team were strengthened. It was not only the prescribing nurses, but also the staff nurses and non-prescribing practice nurse who were included in these sessions, and they also contributed their opinions and ideas on nurse prescribing. Being accountable for our prescribing decisions made us reflect more on our professional practice and our holistic approach to patient care.

Clinical supervision was a recommendation of the evaluation study of nurse prescribing (Luker et al. 1997) and we found this beneficial. The intention of clinical supervision is to allow nurses to reflect on their practice in an analytical way, thus developing knowledge and improving their competence in specific areas of work. Improvements in patient care and sharing 'best practice' can only be achieved if nurses are able to reflect on their professional practice in order to determine what was good about the situation as well as areas for potential improvements. Issues for reflection would encompass not only prescribing practice but also issues such as record keeping, ethical considerations, time management and caseload management. With the extension of nurse prescribing, both clinical supervision and peer review offer an ideal forum for shared learning.

> Group supervision allows all participants in a non-threatening environment, to critically review practice in order to develop their knowledge and skills to meet the patients needs more effectively.
> (Castille 1996)

Despite the initial anxieties and pressures resulting from piloting this project, prescribing very quickly became a routine part of our role and was easily absorbed into working practice. The following text will look at prescribing from a district nurse and then a health visitor perspective.

District nurse

As the district nurse attached to Dr Saul's practice, I was used to making clinical decisions about treatments and initiating prescriptions for the GP to sign, and I agree with the statement in the Crown Report (DoH 1989):

> The nurse who plans and carries through a programme of care and has continuing contact with the patient is uniquely placed to make an accurate assessment of that patient's needs and is the person who should take responsibility for her decisions.
>
> (para 1.18, p. 17)

I started to prescribe on 4 October 1994, and the benefits to me and to the patients were felt immediately.

Time-saving

Time is precious to nurses and patients alike. Not having to go backwards and forwards to the surgery or stand outside the doctor's room to get his signature saves both the doctor's and the nurse's time. Treatments are therefore commenced more quickly, giving a better service to the patients. An example of this is Mrs Brown (not her real name), who was discharged from hospital to a residential home on Friday afternoon. She was a diabetic, new to insulin. She was catheterised and was on twice-daily insulin injections. I visited Mrs Brown at 5.00 p.m. to give her insulin injection and found that she had been discharged with just two insulin syringes and one night drainage bag. At 5.00 p.m. on Friday, this would have caused difficulties for the nurse, doctor and patient in trying to get the necessary equipment from the surgery to last over the weekend. I was able to prescribe the insulin syringes and the drainage bags immediately, with much relief on the part of the care staff and the patient, and saving time for all concerned.

Stockpiling

Prior to nurse prescribing, the delay in getting prescriptions would often lead to patients stockpiling dressings or other products for fear of 'running out'. I am now able to prescribe more appropriate amounts, and there is therefore less waste. It was nearly 12 months before I needed to prescribe a dressing pack for one lady on my caseload: she had 48 in stock, and we only used one dressing pack per week.

Increased concordance

The nurse often has more time than the doctor to explain how to take medication or how to use a product, and this may lead to better compliance. I visited a 65-year-old gentleman who had suffered a cerebrovascular accident and had been discharged from hospital two days previously. He had made a good recovery and had regained much of his independence. His main problem was pain in his affected arm, for which he was taking Co-dydramol, two tablets four times a day. One of the side-effects of these tablets is constipation, of which this gentleman was complaining. After advising about his diet, I also recommended an osmotic laxative, which he then said he had taken before without success. After deeper discussion, he revealed that he had taken one dose at night and had expected to have a bowel movement the following morning. When this did not happen, he had decided it was 'no good'. I prescribed the laxative and explained that it would take 48 hours to work and that he would need to drink extra fluids. He would need to take the laxative regularly for as long as he needed the analgesics. When this gentleman understood the reason for his constipation and how this could be overcome by taking the laxative properly, he complied with the treatment, and, by also including fruit and fibre in his diet, his problem was solved.

Cost awareness

As prescribers, we have definitely become more aware of costs, and, while the aim of the scheme is not to save money but to give a better service to patients and enhance the nurse's role (Cumber-lege 1995), I felt that the cost implication would be a major issue in determining the success or failure of the pilot. By prescribing more appropriate amounts and cheaper products, where appropriate, we actually achieved a cost saving in Bolton.

Continuity of care

Nurse prescribing has improved the care given to our patients and families. Patients like continuity of care, and the nurse–patient relationship has improved. Consider, for example, Mrs Smith (not her real name), a 56-year-old lady with terminal cancer. She was very poorly and in the late stages of her illness. On visiting Mrs Smith on Sunday morning, I found that she had been very uncomfortable all night and had not passed urine for 24 hours. She had not wanted to call out the doctor as he had visited the day before and she feared it would be a 'rota doctor' who did not know her. On examination, her bladder was very distended, and she was obviously retaining urine. I phoned the doctor to discuss Mrs Smith's condition; he was happy for me to catheterise the patient. The prescription for the necessary items was written. Mr Smith went to the pharmacy while I was attending to his wife, and within 45 minutes Mrs Smith was catheterised, her relief being very satisfying to see. The continuity of care at this stage of Mrs Smith's illness was very important to her, and being able to identify the problem, plan, implement and evaluate the care, without needing a visit from a doctor whom she had never seen before, improved her sense of well-being. Other benefits could also be seen from this case: the time saved for the doctor, who did not need to visit just to prescribe the necessary equipment; for the nurse, who did not have to return to the patient after the doctor had visited; for the patient, who did not have to wait too long for treatment to be commenced.

Health promotion

Noack (1987) defines health promotion as a personal approach to individual behaviour change in response to health education. Nurse prescribing has led to increased opportunities for health promotion, for example with regard to bowel management. Rather than prescribing a laxative, time will be taken to discuss diet and lifestyle, and, with encouragement and monitoring, a prescription is sometimes unnecessary. The only concern about nurse prescribing voiced by the doctors at our practice was with regard to the prescribing of laxatives and the fear that a serious condition could remain undetected. The team discussed this at length and agreed that good communication between nurses and doctors was vital. Since the start of nurse prescribing, communication has vastly improved, and the team has been strengthened because of it.

Health visitor

My prescribing anxieties initially centred around the actual writing of the prescription, although I was well aware that, as professionals, we initiate a wide range of treatments and prescriptions; my confidence in relation to nursing assessment and diagnosis seemed to diminish when I realised that I would be totally responsible for the episode of care when signing the prescription. I was conscious of the fact that it is not just the issue of prescribing, but also the professional accountability that goes with the prescribing, that is important. Although, in the past, I considered the ethical, legal and accountability issues when providing care for patients, I often did so subconsciously. One of the major professional benefits for me now is that I do consider all aspects of my duty of care, not just in relation to prescribing; also, through reflective practice, I re-evaluate a larger percentage of my professional roles and responsibilities. Murphy and Atkins (1994) define the reflective process, suggesting that:

> Because reflection involves exploration of a unique situation, new knowledge may be generated. Reflection therefore has the potential to address the problems of practice in a way that the application of technical rational approaches alone do not.
>
> (p. 13)

The following case studies (names have been changed to protect the identities of the clients and maintain confidentiality) allow the reader to recognise reflection in practice, approaches to care and the professional autonomy that has been gained through nurse prescribing.

Case study 1

Melissa, aged 2 months, attended the surgery for her primary course of immunisations. Carole, her mother, was very anxious regarding any possible side-effects. Melissa was Carole's first baby, and this was adding to her anxiety. Carole was a young single parent and doubted she would be able to cope in an emergency should there be any complications following immunisation.

Nursing actions and outcome

Descriptions of the vaccines offered were given to Carole, who decided that Melissa was to have oral polio and the combined injection of diphtheria, tetanus, pertussis and Hib.

Possible reactions to vaccines were carefully explained to Carole, and local reaction at the injection site and the possibility of systemic febrile illness were detailed. Any questions Carole asked were answered openly and honestly. Reassurance was given to Carole that not all babies suffer these reactions, and she was also advised to give paracetamol oral suspension to Melissa in the event of febrile illness. Carole asked if I could give her some paracetamol, so I wrote a prescription for paracetamol oral suspension, 2.5 ml to be given 6-hourly to a maximum of two doses.

I had established prior to vaccination that Melissa was well, had not had any previous injections and had never had any other treatment for any other conditions. I also explained to Carole the signs and symptoms she should look for if febrile illness occurred. The management of febrile illness was also discussed, for example giving fluids, avoiding too much body contact and wearing cool cotton clothing. Carole was advised to use a syringe when administering the paracetamol and I also advised Carole to make a note of the time of administration and what to expect from the treatment: relief from pain and a lowering of temperature. Carole was also assured that, if she was worried about Melissa's condition or she did not feel that the baby's temperature was under control, despite using paracetamol and other management techniques, she should seek the advice of the GP. If Melissa were seen by the doctor, Carole was to show the doctor the medicine prescribed and also state what had already been administered and when. This would avoid any confusion if another prescription were given for paracetamol by any other name, for example Calpol. The medication prescribed was recorded in the GP records and the child health record. Verbal instructions on management were reinforced in writing by way of the parent-held record.

The result

Melissa had a slight temperature; Carole gave one dose of paracetamol suspension and no further treatment was required. I felt that, in prescribing the paracetamol, I had made the right clinical decision. I was advocating the use of the medication during the consultation. When asked whether I could supply it, I felt more confident knowing that Carole would have the recommended medication, dose and application to treat febrile illness should it occur.

Case study 2

Mrs Bates attended a local cytology clinic for which I am responsible. She was a 46-year-old lady who had attended for a routine smear. During the assessment and screening, she declared that she had had vaginal and anal itching for 18 months. Mrs Bates had been seen by the GP but was reluctant to describe her symptoms fully as the GP was male and she was embarrassed. No cause for the itching was determined, and the patient had used various over-the-counter creams to try to alleviate the itch. Mrs Bates was currently using Locan, which was proving ineffective in relieving symptoms, especially at night when the itching was disturbing her sleep.

Nursing actions

During the procedure of taking the smear, I noted the areas of skin excoriation around the vulva and anal area; there was no evidence of acute infection, but I observed that Mrs Bates had threadworms. Once the smear was completed, I asked her if she had had a urine test recently. This was to try to exclude diabetes as an underlying cause for the pruritus. She said that she had had two urine tests, both of which were normal. The patient was not currently taking any oral medication and had no irregular bowel symptoms. I explained to Mrs Bates that she had threadworms; this was done sensitively and Mrs Bates was reassured that they could be treated easily and effectively. There was no need to go back to the GP at this stage.

Treatment

Mrs Bates lived with her husband. I explained the cause and treatment of threadworms and advised that both Mr and Mrs Bates should receive treatment. Both adults paid for prescriptions, and I therefore advised them to buy piperazine and senna powders over the counter. Having explained the cycle of transfer for threadworms, Mrs Bates was also advised to wash her hands and scrub her fingernails prior to eating or preparing food, and always after using the toilet. I suggested that she have a bath in the mornings to remove any new eggs laid overnight. If the sole cause of the pruritus were threadworms, the symptoms should disappear following treatment. If the symptoms persisted, it was suggested that she consult the GP for further investigations.

Reflecting back on this consultation, I feel that my assessment, history taking and diagnosis were within my remit as a competent practitioner. I also feel that the situation needed a sensitive approach to prevent causing the patient unnecessary distress. My decision not to prescribe was justified; I do not feel it would have been ethical to prescribe when an over-the-counter purchase was much cheaper. I did, however, give a detailed explanation of the usage of the medication and also the expected outcomes.

Case study 3

Jonathan attended surgery with his mother, Ann, for a routine child development assessment. He was 3 years old. During the assessment, I noted Jonathan frequently scratching his head. When I mentioned this to his mother, she agreed that I should look at Jonathan's hair. I noted that he was infested with live head lice. Ann's head was also checked and she too had live lice.

Nursing actions and evaluation

I prescribed Malathion Alcoholic Lotion 0.5% in line with the currently recommended mosaic treatment regime. I issued a prescription for Jonathan but recommended that Ann buy the product, as it would be cheaper for her to do so than paying for the prescription. Neither Ann nor Jonathan suffered from asthma or eczema so there were no contraindications to using an alcoholic solution. I advised Ann on correct usage and to follow the written instructions carefully. The myths regarding head lice were dispelled and management techniques to complement medication were discussed with regard to grooming techniques to prevent re-infestation. Ann was advised to inform the nursery that she had effectively treated Jonathan's head lice. If she needed any further help she could contact me at the health centre.

Case study 4

Mrs Cotes attended the well-baby clinic with her 6-week-old daughter, Bethany. Discussion took place regarding Bethany's progress in relation to development and feeding. Mrs Cotes reported that Bethany was unsettled following some feeds, particularly in the evenings. Bethany was taking 6 oz formula feeds. She tolerated the amount well; however, Mrs Cotes reported that Bethany cried in the evenings and was drawing her legs up. Colic was discussed, and we decided that the use of an activated dimeticone agent ('colic' drops) prior to feeds would be appropriate to complement management techniques. While the benefit of such a product is not proved by research evidence (Lucassen et al. 1998) my own professional assessment of this family led me to believe that in this situation 'colic' drops would be helpful. During the visit, I also noted that Bethany had oral thrush; the cause and management of the condition was explained to Mrs Cotes.

Treatment

Bethany needed a prescription for nystatin 100,000 units/ml and activated dimeticone. As a nurse prescriber, I was able to provide a prescription for nystatin; however, due to the limited NPF, I was unable to prescribe the 'colic' drops. This necessitated Mrs Cotes arranging to see her GP, resulting in an unnecessary consultation that delayed Bethany's treatment and was a waste of Mrs Cotes' and the GP's time.

I hope that these case studies show how, in my position as a health visitor, prescribing has enhanced the opportunities for working in partnership with patients and clients in the effective treatment and management of the conditions described. Chayass (1992) stresses that working in partnership improves the holistic approach to care by allowing an equal sharing of power within the relationship. As Playle and Keeley (1998, p. 310) note:

> Patients need to be viewed as active participants rather than passive recipients in their own health care.

Management techniques have been highlighted in all cases, which should improve effective treatment and prevent the need for unnecessary consultations with the GP, or repeat prescriptions because treatment has failed.

In each of the cases outlined, I feel I can justify my practice in relation to assessment, diagnosis and treatment. Doctors are taught to use a medical model to enable them to reach a diagnosis and provide treatment; however, as nurses, we are taught to use a nursing/social model. I believe that nurse prescribing allows us to combine the two, and thus the patient receives appropriate care – which may not always result in the issuing of a prescription – promoting a holistic approach to the delivery of care. There is evidence in literature that identifies the dissatisfaction many people experience when trying to communicate with doctors (Cartwright 1967; Gregory 1978; Ley 1988). Byrne and Lang (1976) conclude in their study that over 60 per cent of doctors gather information, analyse and probe to fit the patient into a medically defined disease category. The patient's involvement in this process of diagnosis is limited. The doctor may make little or no attempt to see the patient's situation from his or her point of view.

I have found that there has been a definite increase in professional autonomy. This has improved teamwork and nurse–patient
relationships, and has allowed me to work as an equal member of
the primary health care team. As a prescriber, I am now more
professionally aware of the safety, ethical and economic issues
involved in prescribing and patient care delivery.

It is recognised by health visitors that there are some omissions
from the NPF, the addition of which would be of benefit in
meeting the needs of clients within the home (Humphries and
Green 2001). Following the consultation on proposals to extend
nurse prescribing (DoH 2000), these are now being addressed
(MCA 2001).

I have no doubts that nurse prescribing has improved professional and client relationships, resulting in a more appropriate use
of professional skills and the enhancement of patient care.

Prescribing difficulties

Historically, nurse prescribing was not without problems, the
main one, initially, being the generic prescribing of wound care
products. Having to write 'vapour permeable adhesive film
dressing' instead of 'OP site' or 'Tegaderm' was impractical and
time consuming. Pharmacists were having great problems with
these prescriptions and needed to know which specific brands
were wanted. Fortunately, since April 1997, it has been acceptable
to use brand names for wound care products, which has saved
time for nurses and helped the pharmacists tremendously.

Another problem was record keeping: having to record every-
thing prescribed in three different places, that is, patient-held
records, the GP's records and nurse records at the health centre,
was time consuming and, for some items, seemed unnecessary.

This was overcome following discussion with the trust and the
GPs. The decision was made that systemic medication was to be
recorded on GP records as soon as possible but that wound care
products and appliances needed only to be recorded on patient-
held records, which are accessible to all health care professionals.

Conclusion

There is no doubt that nurse prescribing is a success. All the community staff involved have commented on the improvement to patient care delivery that nurse prescribing has made. Nurses have proved that they can prescribe cost-effectively. The time-saving, continuity of care, better compliance and opportunities for health promotion are ensuring a more responsive and efficient service to our patients and clients. Prescribing has improved both job satisfaction and professional autonomy for the nurses involved.

> Our goal must be to ensure, eventually, that every nurse in the country who is suitably trained and who is committed to nurse prescribing should be allowed to do so, in the interests of patient care and the nursing profession.
>
> (Cumberlege 1997)

As nurse prescribers, we hope that this comes to fruition sooner rather than later, enabling other nurses to experience the professional benefits that prescribing brings. Being involved in this major advance for nursing has certainly increased our job satisfaction, and it is very rewarding to hear our colleagues say, 'What on earth did we do before?'

References

Byrne, P. and Lang, B. (1976) *Doctors Talking to Patients.* HMSO, London.

Carlisle, D. (1989) Prescribing charge. *Community Outlook,* November: 26.

Cartwright, A. (1967) *Patients and their Doctors.* Routledge, London.

Castille, K. (1996) Clinical supervision from rhetoric to accident and emergency practice. *Accident and Emergency Nursing,* **4**: 2–4.

Chayass, J. (1992) New dimensions of experiments in nursing. *Journal of Advanced Nursing,* **17**: 1–2.

Cumberlege, J. (1995) Sharing prescribing power. *Community Nursing,* **1**(1).

Cumberlege, J. (1997) Nurse prescribing must not be for trading. *Nurse Prescriber Newsletter,* **5**: 1.

DoH (1989) *Report of the Advisory Group on Nurse Prescribing* (Crown Report). DoH, London.

DoH (1999) *Review of Prescribing, Supply and Administration of Medicines* (Crown II Report). DoH, London.

DoH (2000) *Consultation on proposals to extend nurse prescribing.* http://www.doh.gov.uk/nurseprescribing/index.htm.

DoH (2001) *Patients to get quicker access to medicines.* Press release: reference 2001/0223. DoH, London.

Gregory, J. (1978) Patients' Attitudes to the Hospital Service. A survey resource paper (No. 5). HMSO, London.

Humphries, J. and Green, E. (2001) The expansion of the *Nurse Prescribers' Formulary. Nurse Prescriber/Community Nurse, 7 (1):* 27–33.

Hunt, J. (1988) Primary nursing: the next challenge. *Nursing Times,* **84**(49): 36, 38.

Kaufman, G. (1996) Nurse Practitioners in general practice: an expanding role. *Nursing Standard,* **11**(8): 44–7.

Ley, P. (1988) *Communicating with Patients. Improving Communication, Satisfaction and Compliance.* Stanley Thornes, Cheltenham.

Lucassen, P., Assendelft, W.J.J., Gubbels, J.W., van Eijk, J.T.M., van Geldrop, W.J. and Knuistingh Neven, A. (1998) Effectiveness of treatments for infantile colic: systematic review. *British Medical Journal,* **316**: 1563–9.

Luker, K.A., Austin, L., Hogg, C., Willock, J., Wright, K. Ferguson, B. Jenkins-Clark, S. and Smith, K. (1997) Evaluation of Nurse Prescribing Final Report: Executive Summary. Unpublished Report.

Medicines Control Agency (2001) *Extended Prescribing of Prescription Only Medicines by Independent Nurse Prescribers.* www.mca.gov.uk.

Murphy, K. and Atkins, S. (1994) Reflection with a practice-led curriculum. In Palmer, A., Burns, S. and Bulman, C. (eds) *Reflective Practice in Nursing.* Blackwell Science, Oxford.

Noack, H. (1987) *Concepts of Health Promotions: Measurement in Health Promotion and Protection.* WHO, Copenhagen, pp. 5–28.

Patterson, C. and Haddad, B. (1992) The advanced nurse practitioner: common attributes. *Journal of Nursing,* **5**(11): 391–8.

Pearson, A. (1987) *Nursing Quality Measurement Quality Assurance Methods for Peer Review.* Wiley, London.

Playle, J. F. and Keeley, P. (1998) Non-compliance and professional power. *Journal of Advanced Nursing,* **27**: 304–11.

Stilwell, B. (1988) Patient attitudes to a highly developed role – the nurse practitioner. *Recent Advances in Nursing,* (21): 82–100.

Tingle, J.H. (1990) Nurses and the Law. *Nursing Times,* **86**(38): 70–2.

Tschudin, V. (1986) *Ethics in Nursing.* Heinemann, London.

Winstanley, F. (1998) Why nurse prescribing is good for you. *Community Nurse,* **4**: 43–4.

9 Will you walk a little faster...?

David Skidmore

This chapter originally borrowed from Dylan Thomas for a title: Do not go Gentle ... Dylan Thomas's poem begs one not to accept death meekly but to rage 'against the dying of the light' (Thomas [1939]1987). While still relevant for nurse prescribing, recent moves and conjectures, even as this chapter is being revised, suggest that Lewis Carroll's ([1865]1968) 'Quadrille' is more appropriate. Nurses, it seems, have to 'rage' in order to develop their role. Green indicates (Chapter 1) that nurse prescribing is not a new idea, originally being mooted some 14 years before the first demonstration sites were announced. The demonstration was running for some four years prior to being rolled out to some nurses. The exclusion of other community nurses makes a significant contribution to the secularisation of nursing.

The practitioner debate categorises nurses in terms of core, specialist and advanced. Core practice, it is suggested, is demonstrated by those skills achieved by way of first-level registration and equips nurses to undertake generalist activities (Poulton 1997). The specialist practitioner should demonstrate higher levels of practice; involving study at degree level (UKCC 1994). The advanced practitioner is still ill defined (UKCC 1996). However, Woods (1998) argues that those nurses who undertake advanced practitioner courses experience difficulty in describing their role. Furthermore they tend to find themselves somewhat alienated from nursing colleagues. It is argued that elevating the status of practice is more than the sum total of courses completed and, if measured only by the level of academic achievement, may be disruptive within a nursing culture. Nurse prescribing could be seen to elevate the practice of an exclusive group of nurses, a group who belong to those categorised as specialist practitioners. The press release (DoH 2001) reinforces this, identifying specialist nurses in A&E, specialist asthma nurses and, on the recommendations of the final report into prescribing (DoH 1999a), other health professionals such as pharmacists, physiotherapists and chiropodists. While I have no problem with extending prescribing to other professionals, the snail-like pace of this roll-out is alarming. Supplementary prescribing (that is, continuing care following clinical assessment by an independent prescriber, such as dose adjustment and repeat prescriptions) has been a feature of nursing, albeit unofficially and illegally, for many years. The aim is to increase the number of independent prescribers in order to free up doctors' time 'allowing them to deal with more serious cases' (DoH 2001). The remit appears to be to identify NHS need, with regard to prescribing, and then identify those professionals (starting with nurses) who will need access to prescribing training. With regard to supplementary (dependent) prescribers the evidence could be collected now. Mental health nurses readily come to mind, particularly those involved in the care of persons with severe and enduring mental illness; similarly nurses working in the care of diabetes, asthma and A&E. All that is needed is an invitation to 'come and join the dance' (Carroll [1865]1968).

Groves (Chapter 2) argues that nursing has advanced considerably in terms of autonomy and practice; I would argue that much of that advancement has taken place at a rapid pace from the 1980s onwards. However, such advancement is not uniform in terms of recognition and it does seem contradictory to recognise all community nurses as specialist practitioners and yet limit nurse prescribing to just two groups. Such limitation has serious implications for the realisation of effective teamwork and a 'seamless' service. Groves quite rightly suggests that nurse prescribing can only be beneficial for the advancement of nursing practice and yet, in terms of its introduction, it may be divisive.

The early 1990s held the promise of a new horizon for nursing: one voice, a voice that would take nursing forward. There really was a possibility that nurses would come together as a unified body. Unfortunately the further development of educational programmes now seems to militate against such unification. The titles specialist and advanced suggest skills beyond those practised by the everyday, common or garden nurse. Indeed, the UKCC (1994) states that the specialist will demonstrate the development of practice through research, improve standards of care through supervised practice and demonstrate higher levels of decision-making. This higher level of practice can only be accessed after first-level registration. Does this suggest, then, that the first-level nurse, with her core skills, is a lesser nurse? Is she enrolled by any other name? Should she forget the art of nursing that is embedded in caring and concentrate on those skills that can claim higher qualifications? Caring, the essence of nursing is very difficult to assess in the academic sense; peers, however, often have an accurate view of what makes a good nurse. There is the rub. If legislation grants more autonomy to one group of nurses there is an inequality that prevents effective peer review.

The current nurse prescribers' course (1995–2001) is only open to health visitors and district nurses (or practice nurses who hold either qualification). One can only speculate as to which other nursing groups will be included – the relevant press releases still refer to specialist nurses and, although there is mention of walk-in clinics, the practice nurse appears to remain excluded from immediate future roll-out. This suggests that these nurses already possess some unique skill or knowledge that places them apart from 'ordinary' nurses. Oddly, Poulton (1997) suggests that it is the practice nurse who holds a more generic role in primary health and yet, unless they hold the HV or DN qualification, they are ineligible for nurse prescriber courses, even though they are (from 1997) recognised as specialist practitioners. Green (Chapter 1) argues that nurse prescribing is a major step forward for nursing and Groves (Chapter 2) that it will help reduce the hours that junior doctors are required to work. Green's comment that this is only the beginning still rings true ... we are still beginning. To be of real benefit to the health service (in its fifty-fifth year) nurse prescribing must be extended to all practitioner nurses (at least) who have been functioning as dependent prescribers for years.

There are thousands of practice nurses who will be denied the right to prescribe and Poulton (1997) reveals that there has been a 300 per cent increase in practice nurses employed in general practice. Indeed, the intensive interest in practice nursing (DoH 1999) suggested that they would be the key workers in community health by the millennium. The situation created by nurse prescribing within practice nursing illuminates the future implications for nursing as a whole. In the pilot sites the situation exists whereby a small number of practice nurses can prescribe but a larger number can not. The licence to prescribe sets a minority of practice nurses apart from their colleagues. There is one school of thought that would argue that practice nurses have always prescribed; but the practice that they put forward as evidence is not autonomous practice, and is also illegal. Nurse prescribers, on the other hand, have government blessing to possess a skill denied to others in their ranks.

Woods (1998) argues that such practices alienate nurses from their colleagues because they are viewed in a different way. The practice and everyday demeanour of the nurse may not change and yet others will perceive them as having changed. The nurse prescriber can maintain her behaviour in identical fashion to her colleagues but need only sign one prescription to be confirmed as different. Mental health nursing offers evidence of how this might develop in practice.

During the 1970s, in the field of psychiatry, two groups of nurses became similarly isolated: community psychiatric nurses and, what were then, behavioural therapists. They were accused of not wanting to be nurses any more, of being mental health visitors or 'wannabe' psychologists. The subsequent alienation led to the formation of their own associations or the joining of more welcoming groups (The British Association of Behavioural Psychotherapy); thereby confirming to onlookers that they were trying to be more than a nurse. In truth these groups were looking for mutual support to help them cope with new nursing developments (Skidmore and Friend 1984).

In practice they unwittingly contributed to the secularisation of psychiatric nursing (Skidmore 1997). The solidarity of psychiatric nurses witnessed during the 1950s and 60s was rapidly becoming a thing of the past. In response to the Community Psychiatric Nurses Association non-CPNs formed the Psychiatric Nurses Association and, although both groups stopped short of the membership monopoly (that is, only permitting membership of one association as in the rules of the medical royal colleges of the 19th century), great rivalries existed. One speculates about how much more secure the future of psychiatric nursing would be today had the solidarity survived. Mental health nursing is on the verge of a manpower crisis within the next ten years (*Journal of Health Service Management* 1997). There has not been the right level of recruitment and retention to offset the impending retirements.

Let us return to nurse prescribing, although the above diatribe is pertinent. Any separation of one nursing group will erode the common identity. It does not take a Marx or Durkheim to theorise about this: the evidence is in our own history. What is so special about health visitors and district nurses that places them in a unique position whereby prescribing licences can be conferred upon them? The NHS Executive (1996) claims that the health visitor role is focused on the wider public health agenda whereas:

> district nurses address clearly defined health needs, largely with the housebound and elderly.

While I can see the rationale for including district nurses into the prescribing team, I could not justify the inclusion of health visitors. I do not seek to denigrate health visiting but view their role in a more proactive sense; they are truly in the front line of prevention for which there are few, if any, prescriptions. Indeed they work in health while most nurses work in illness. It could be argued that they have moved out of nursing per se; in fact it is only with the new specialist community awards that nursing has crept back into the title. Indeed, there is now talk of locating health visitors under Home Office control (Coombes 1998). Singling out one group of nurses in this way is, of course, unfair; they, like any qualified nurse, should be allowed to prescribe. Please note the 'any qualified nurse'. Nurse prescribing has commenced the slow roll-out and, as originally stated, nursing is going to enter an *Animal Farm*-type phase:

> All nurses are equal
> but some nurses are more
> equal than others.
>
> (after Orwell, 1945)

Should extending prescribing roles to other professionals occur before including all qualified nurses, the message will be all the stronger. Nurse prescribing can only be good for nursing. Green (Chapter 1) argues that it is seen as a valuable component to community nursing. It could be so much more in terms of unifying nursing. In the midst of confusion by the professional boards with regard to what specialist practice is (Mahoney 1997), the profession is still willing to confer an aegis of speciality on certain groups. While there is dissent (Jones and Gough, 1997), the professional body appears to be going gentle into that good night and government sources practising the Quadrille (a step-by-step approach). The major outcome will be that these two groups will be more specialist than the other specialist practitioners since only two of the eight specialist community branches will be allowed to prescribe. Since the UKCC decided in March 1997 not to establish explicit standards for advanced practice, it is difficult to know how to locate this élite workforce. Certainly it will add to the confusion of attempting to define specialist practitioners and government-speak persists in talking about specialist nurses. The paradox here is that the ENB has already defined specialist practitioner awards, of which the general practice nurse's is one, and yet other than as health visitors and district nurses they appear not to figure in the immediate future plans. Confusing indeed!

Castledine (quoted in Mahoney 1997) argues that specialist practitioner status is reflected in clinical skill, not courses completed; and that it is practice led not education led. Unfortunately his argument, while being laudable, is not supported by events. Consider nurse prescribing as a practitioner skill. Quite rightly, it should be assessed through practice: only then can it be practice led. It is currently indeed a reflection of courses completed: health visiting or district nursing plus nurse prescribers' course equals super-specialist practitioner. One could also question whether or not the current arrangements to become a community specialist practitioner are practice led. Nurses must still complete a recognised course; demonstration of experience and clinical skill is not sufficient. Castledine (quoted in Mahoney 1997, p. 8) goes on to suggest that:

> We have got to develop a framework for evaluation or the term (specialist practitioner) could fall into disrepute.

Given that more balls are thrown into the juggling act (almost every week it seems) forming committees to develop such frameworks is rather futile. There is now a call for nurse anaesthetists (Audit Commission 1997); where will these fit into the specialist versus advanced debate and will they have prescribing powers of a dependent or independent nature? All the committees in the world are doomed to failure when trying to unravel this Gordian knot of nursing since they have yet to define and agree just what a nurse is. On the positive side inroads have been made since this chapter was initially written. *Making a Difference* (DoH 1999b) and *Fitness for Practice* (UKCC 1999) recognise the practice element of nursing and invest in the importance of this for nursing. It does appear that an agreement regarding what nurses should be able to do on qualification may be near. However, nurse prescribing adds more strands to the knot if it is to be reserved for an élite group of nurses and other professions. It should be a basic skill of all first-level nurses. After all, the *Formulary* as it stands is hardly earth-shatteringly dangerous so why are the Department of Health and the professional bodies so cautious about its introduction as a supplementary skill? Added to this conundrum is the fact that one of the groups entitled to enter nurse prescribing courses (health visitors) is under threat nationwide. Throughout November and December 1997, *Nursing Times* carried news reports of massive redundancies in health visiting. Add the point that nurses should take over half of the GP's workload (Nuffield Trust 1997) and the knot becomes tighter and more difficult to untie. Obviously, if nurses are to take on some of the functions of GPs, they must prescribe; yet the nurse closest to the GP role is, as yet, disqualified from entering the prescribers' course.

The starting point to this debate is that all qualified nurses should be licensed to prescribe. This is the only tenet that will recognise all nurses as equal. It is also the only starting point that will permit sense to be made of specialist and advanced practitioners, especially if one accepts that such titles are won through a practice-led framework. A staged recognition of basic practical skills (and prescribing is a basic skill) cannot work. Imagine the newly qualified medical doctor who has to refer a patient to a colleague for a prescription! It is quite ludicrous.

There is, however, a negative aspect contained in the process of rolling out nurse prescribing to all nurses. It will, undoubtedly, add to the blurring of doctor–nurse roles, particularly if the prescribing nurse is one of the new 'consultants'. Giving added responsibility to nurses, in whatever environment, has the consequence of nurses having to prioritise their duties. Some activities will be seen as being of less importance with the result that some nursing skills will be marginalised at a time when recognition for basic nursing skills is dawning. The major benefit of basic nursing skills is that they facilitate nurse–patient communication. Certainly supplementary prescribing can create a pencil and paper exercise and, consequently, the greatest danger is that prescribing will form a barrier to nurse–patient communication. In the past the nurse was seen as a carer and this facilitated patient communication. It will change the way in which nurses are seen by the public. They will, indeed, become demi-gods in the way that doctors are gods. Obviously, this will not be a deliberate act, on the part of the nurse, but the fact that she has a legal right to prescribe will suggest that she has more power than the average nurse. Nurse prescribing is not necessarily a bad thing although its step by step roll-out could be devastating for nursing. There is a lot to lose ... the art and practice of nursing being paramount. If nurse prescribing must be introduced, then all qualified nurses should be allowed to prescribe. Obviously there will need to be regulation of independent prescribers and, quite rightly, this should be limited to those nurses with specialist skills; however all qualified nurses could function effectively as supplementary prescribers. Nurses rarely take blood samples now because phlebotomists were created; bed-making has also become a back page of nursing history. If nurses are not careful, some future historian could well be asking: where did all the nurses go? There is an aggressive movement to institute doctors' assistants and many nurses support this. Nurse prescribing facilitates this new identity of the hybrid nurse casting off the mantle of nursing and taking on the partial cloak of the doctor. On the positive side it could render the specialist practitioner debate redundant, on the negative side it could signal the death knell of nursing as we know it in the UK. This may well be compounded when prescribing licences are rolled out to other professionals. There will be a group of health care professionals who are independent prescribers, capable of clinical assessment and prescribing a course of treatment, and a group of supplementary prescribers who are responsible for continuing care. It is not a very long step to then recommend that independent prescribers can take on more of the junior doctor's role.

Nurse prescribing could have been used to help define primary health care nursing. Although it has been argued that it should be accessible by all qualified nurses, in reality it has been and will be conferred on the few (since roll-out began only 18,000 practitioners have completed preparation by January 2001 (Association for Nurse Prescribing 2001)); had it been thought through it could have unified nursing practice in primary health care. There is a need to revisit the issue of what is required in primary health nursing, but that need not exclude health visitors and district nurses. Certainly it should not require replacing nurses with assistant doctors. Nurses are nurses; if they lose sight of that fact then the whole arena of health care becomes a circus. It is argued above that all qualified nurses possess the experience and ability to prescribe dependently. Nursing is essentially a practitioner role, it should, indeed, be practice led. Nurse prescribing is a part of practice, not a right claimed by having done the right courses. While it is logical that nurses prescribe it is criminal that nursing is fragmented by limiting supplementary prescribing.

The benefits of extending the role of the nurse (archaic term) must not be denied. It will offer more accessibility to the patient, save doctors' time and be economically sound. All of this is good. What is not understandable is why only a small proportion of nurses are being given prescribing rights when the argument for giving all nurses prescribing powers is so sound. The DoH (2001) press release states that extending the scope of prescribing by nurses will, 'free up doctors' time ...' Why not, then, extend this to all qualified nurses? The plan is to produce two types of prescribers and, as argued above, there is understandable caution about extending independent prescribing status. Certainly this is an area where specialist clinical knowledge needs to be identified first. The same argument cannot apply to supplementary prescribers since it can, in reality, only be relevant to their sphere of practice. There will be a period of evaluation, one hopes, before permits are issued for independent prescribing by other professions.

There is a precarious future for nursing if nurse prescribing is to be confined to élite groups. It transcends the specialist practitioner debate in that it clearly identifies a group of nurses who have 'higher' skills than the rest. Nurse prescribing has been educationally led, there has been little objection from practitioners; this does not bode well for the future of nursing. The professional bodies have been complacent about the form of assessment for nurse prescribing: a classroom-based examination. The educationalists involved in the pilot scheme wanted a practical aspect to the examination but were overruled. Hardly a practice-led venture!

It would seem that the future of community nursing has been identified. It lies with the practice nurse (who is currently being upgraded to specialist practitioner). The evidence is offered by the Department of Health in the publication *Practice Nursing: A Changing Role to Meet Changing Needs* (Poulton 1997). A major role for the practice nurse is seen as health maintenance and includes management of conditions such as:

● asthma, diabetes, hypertension
● monitoring of epilepsy, arthritis, anaemia, coronary heart disease, mental illness
● treatment/management of leg ulcers, wound management, eating disorders

all conditions currently being considered in relation to extending the *Nurses' Formulary* (MCA 2001). How can it be, then, that the very nurses identified by Poulton (1997) as being in the frontline of primary care are excluded from nurse prescribing courses? (only 14 per cent of practice nurses have a recognised community nursing qualification). Come to think of it, how do you recognise a community nursing qualification?

So what implication does nurse prescribing have for the future of nursing? It can be the saviour and equally the executioner of nursing. It can provide a starting point for basic nursing skills to continue and further develop and, subsequently, explain specialist and advanced practitioners (should independent prescribing be rolled out to nurses). It will certainly be divisive unless all qualified nurses can prescribe independently.

References

Association for Nurse Prescribing (2001) *Nurse Prescribing Handbook*. Emap Healthcare, London.
Audit Commission (1997) *Anaesthesia Under Examination*. Audit Commission, London.

Carroll, L. ([1865]1968) *The Adventures of Alice in Wonderland.* Penguin, Harmondsworth.

Coombes, R. (1998) Shock plan for health visitors. *Nursing Times,* **94**(27): 5.

DoH (1999a) *Review of Prescribing, Supply and Administration of Medicines. Final Report.* DoH, London.

DoH (1999b) *Making a Difference.* DoH, London.

DoH (2001) *Patients to get quicker access to medicines.* Press release: reference 2001/0223. DoH, London.

Jones, M. and Gough, P. (1997) Nurse prescribing – why has it taken so long? *Nursing Standard,* **11**(20): 39–42.

Journal of Health Service Management (1997). News. **107**(5542): 7.

Mahoney, C. (1997) Bid to end confusion over specialist practice. *Nursing Times,* **93**(50): 8.

Medicines Control Agency (2001) *Extended Prescribing of Prescription Only Medicines by Independent Nurse Prescribers.* www.mca.gov.uk.

NHS Executive (1996) *Primary Care: The Future.* NHSE, Leeds.

Nuffield Trust (1997) *The Physician Workforce in the UK.* Nuffield Trust, London.

Nursing Times (1998). This week. *Nursing Times,* **94**(27): 5.

Orwell, G. (1945) *Animal Farm.* Secker & Warburg, London.

Poulton, B. (1997) *Practice Nursing: A Changing Role to Meet Changing Needs.* DoH, London.

Skidmore, D. (1997) *The Decline of the British Nurse.* Third International Conference, Martin, Slovakia.

Skidmore, D. and Friend, W. (1984) Muddling through. *Nursing Times, Community Outlook,* 9 May: 179–81.

Thomas, D. ([1939]1987) Do not go gentle into that good night. In Wain, J. (ed.) *Oxford Library of English Poetry.* Oxford University Press, Oxford.

UKCC (1994) *The Council's Standards for Education and Practice following Registration.* Registrar's Letter. UKCC, London.

UKCC (1996) PREP: *The Nature of Advanced Practice.* CC/96146. UKCC, London.

UKCC (1999) *Fitness for Practice.* UKCC, London.

Woods, L. (1998) Reconstructing nursing: a study of role transition in advanced nursing practice. Unpublished PhD thesis. Keele University.

10

Nurse prescribing case studies

Jennifer L. Humphries

This chapter presents a range of case studies that illustrate some examples of nurse prescribing situations. Readers may find it useful to work through the complete scenario – from assessment to evaluation. For each of the case studies, several points have been picked out for discussion. These are not intended to be exhaustive but rather to present a range of issues that the nurse prescriber may need to consider. The complexity of factors that impinge on the nurse prescribing role is clearly demonstrated.

Case study 1

Frances, aged 38 years, attends the well person's clinic. During the consultation she informs the nurse of a recurrence of vaginal thrush that was previously successfully treated with pessaries. However, on this occasion she notes that there is a mild rash in the groin area and perineum.

It is vital that the nurse prescriber determines what the patient means by recurrence, that is, how many times she has had the problem and in what timescale. Blenkinsop and Paxton (1998) note that if a patient has had more than two episodes within the last six months a referral to a doctor is necessary. Young (2001) advises that referral to a sexual health clinic is often appropriate in people under the age of 25 years; and when there has been a recent change in sexual partner or sexual contact with a partner with a known sexually transmitted infection. The suggestion in the scenario is that this is the second episode. Assessment issues are to determine the history of the past infection and the presenting complaint. People with a lower resistance to infection, such as those with diabetes, may be prone to fungal infections (Landsell-Smith 2001) and a urine or blood test would be prudent.

In determining a diagnosis the question is raised as to whether the nurse accepts the patient's own assessment of the problem. It will be useful to establish who diagnosed the first episode. If this was assessed and diagnosed by a doctor and the patient recognises the same symptoms, the nurse prescriber will have more confidence than if Frances had merely discussed the problem with a friend who offered lay advice. A decision to examine the patient may also depend on the nature of the nurse prescriber's role. For example, practice nurses and family planning nurses routinely undertake vaginal examination whereas this is unusual for health visitors.

The cost of a prescription has to be considered and in this situation it is likely that advising Frances to buy a product is the most cost-effective option both for the patient and the NHS.

Case study 2

Sarah is a district nurse working on the evening service and is a competent and confident nurse prescriber. She has found her practice has been enhanced by her ability to prescribe for patients and during her career as a prescriber she has used most parts of the NPF. She is aware of her professional responsibility and ensures that her practice is regularly updated by attending study days and making regular visits to the library. She has recently taken on a part-time job as a deputy matron of a small nursing home, situated in the same community trust that she works for. During a shift at the home, Jenny, a patient with multiple sclerosis, complains of a sore mouth. Sarah undertakes a full nursing assessment and diagnoses oral thrush. She writes a prescription for Jenny for 28 nystatin pastilles 100,000 units.

What Sarah has done is illegal. Although she is registered with the UKCC as a nurse prescriber she is only able to prescribe in her role as a district nurse. Prescribing is part of normal practice for Sarah when working as a district nurse so the community trust, as her employer, is vicariously liable for her actions. However, she does not have the permission of her employers at the nursing home so they will not accept vicarious liability.

Case study 3

During a home visit to Rita and her 5-week-old daughter Fiona, Rita informs the nurse prescriber that although her episiotomy scar has healed she is experiencing mild to moderate perineal pain.

While damage to the perineum is not an inevitable part of childbirth, Glossop (1996) suggests that almost 80 per cent of women do experience some trauma, whether from episiotomy, tears or from bruising and swelling. The associated pain can dominate the postnatal period (Steen and Cooper 1998) and affect a woman's normal activities such as walking, breastfeeding and even carrying her baby. Glossop (1996) reports that recovery time can take up to six months and perhaps longer for some women, although the majority of mothers begin to feel that their perineum is back to normal by six weeks after the birth. Rita should be reassured that 'there is great variation in the rate and nature of perineal healing' (Glossop 1996, p. 98). The assessment should exclude infection, and pain relief by local methods can be explored. Sleep and Grant (1988) and Glossop (1996) discuss the benefits of paracetamol for the relief of perineal pain. Interestingly Glossop (1996) reports that about a quarter of women in a study by the National Childbirth Trust turned down offers of oral analgesia and she speculates that this may have been due to concern about the effect on the baby. Rita should therefore be reassured about the safety of paracetamol when breastfeeding and its properties in relieving perineal pain, thus allowing her to enjoy her baby.

Case study 4

As a new prescriber Gill welcomes the opportunity to be able to prescribe emollient bath additives as several clients have dry skin conditions, including dermatitis, eczema, pruritis in the elderly. A pharmaceutical representative (rep) from Best Laboratories (a well-known multinational company) calls to see all the nurse prescribers at the health centre to extol the virtues of Smooth and Silky bath additive. He has several free samples of the product for Gill to give to patients and clients. He also gives Gill some full-size bottles for her own use (she suffers from occasional eczema).

In addition the rep gives Gill a very attractive diary cover, pens and a mug, all bearing the Smooth and Silky name and logo. There are patient leaflets explaining some of the different common skin problems offering very good general advice about skin care. The product is mentioned only briefly at the end of the leaflet although the logo is prominent on all pages. The rep invites all the prescribing nurses to a study evening at a local hotel, where a buffet supper will be provided. He tells Gill that the evening will give an update on current research about skin problems including the research undertaken showing the benefits of Smooth and Silky. Finally, he tells Gill that if she writes ten prescriptions for Smooth and Silky in the next six weeks she will be entitled to a free day at a local (highly prestigious) health farm and beauty salon.

To some extent personal and professional experiences will be influential in the way that Gill deals with the issues presented in the scenario. However several things can assist in the decisions taken. The UKCC (1992) *Code of Professional Conduct* provides nurses with guidance for conduct. Of particular relevance is clause 16 that states:

> Ensure that your registration status is not used in the promotion of commercial products or other services, declare any financial or other interests in relevant organisations providing such goods or services and ensure that your professional judgement is not influenced by any commercial considerations.

It is worth noting that advertising is a powerful medium for 'getting the message across' in all sorts of situations and it is used extensively in the developed world. Aronson (1980, p. 52) notes:

> Manufacturers of nearly identical products (aspirin for example) spend vast amounts of money to persuade us to buy the product in *their* package. This influence can be very subtle indeed, even unintentional.

Acknowledging the potential of this persuasion is useful, and should be considered when using material with a name or logo on. Gill may not be intending to promote a product but it is worth remembering that patients and clients too can be inadvertently influenced. Many trusts provide their employees with clear guidelines concerning contact with reps (Lipley 2000; Magee

2000) and with the acceptance of 'gifts' or products. There may be legal as well as ethical dimensions, for example in the use of 'samples' (whether small or full size) to treat a patient or in a 'try before you buy capacity'.

A recent study by Hallet et al. (2000) into the processes involved in clinical decision-making noted that community nurses drew on a range of sources for information, and that included drug company representatives. Some of the participants thought that information from such sources was useful because it was up to date although 'others were suspicious of the information because of its doubtful basis in research' (p. 790). Interestingly the researchers noted that some participants had commented that that since the start of nurse prescribing they had received more attention from the reps.

Case study 5

Baby Matthew is five weeks old. He is fully breastfed and settled and contented between feeds. He is gaining weight satisfactorily. His mother, Teresa, is concerned that the baby is constipated because he is having his bowels open infrequently and irregularly (approximately every 3–4 days). Teresa's mother has told her that everyone should pass a motion every day and that Matthew is constipated. The health visitor has spoken to Teresa about this on several occasions, at home, in the clinic and at the postnatal support group that she facilitates.

Teresa has also seen her GP, who examined the baby and said he was a fit healthy boy. She has now contacted another doctor in the practice, who refers mother and baby back to the health visitor telling her to prescribe a laxative for Matthew, and that this is the information that he has given to Teresa.

This case study raises several issues in respect of the nurse prescriber's accountability. The aim is to act in the best interests of the clients. Although the baby is not constipated and is clearly well and thriving, his mother also has needs that must be addressed. Teresa's feelings need to be fully explored, conflicting advice from health professionals can add to her anxiety. The health visitor should reflect on their previous contacts since it is clear Teresa's worries have not been abated. If, following discussion of Teresa's perception of constipation, she remains unconvinced, the options of suggesting an alteration to Teresa's diet or of giving Matthew cool boiled water between feeds may be considered. A prescribing decision – and this includes the decision not to prescribe – has to include the client. It may be that if Teresa feels she is 'doing' something her anxiety will lessen and although neither option would seem necessary they are both innocuous solutions that would not bring into question a nurse's accountability, which prescribing laxatives inappropriately certainly would.

New mothers often welcome advice and support from their own mother and it is vital that the relationship is not damaged by what the nurse prescriber says. A diplomatic approach is essential. It may be worthwhile seeing Teresa's mother or perhaps leaving pertinent literature.

It is possible that Teresa has misinterpreted what the second GP has said, since it would seem strange that if his assessment determined that a laxative was indicated, he did not prescribe. Gentle exploration of Teresa's perception of the consultation is worthy of consideration. If her account is accurate there is a need to speak to the GP. He has to be aware that nurse prescribers will not prescribe a product as a result of another's assessment. Moreover, the health visitor has a duty of care to her client, and discussion with the GP of the normal bowel habits of a breastfed infant may correct any misconceptions that the GP has. Again, effective interpersonal skills are required to avoid the danger of appearing critical of a doctor's competence.

Case study 6

Chrissy and Alf are a couple in their 30s who have moderate learning difficulties. They live in the ground floor flat of a dwelling that houses two other people with learning difficulties. Since Chrissy and Alf's son Ben was born 18 months ago there have been numerous support services involved to help the family. Chrissy and Alf attend the local Family Centre three times a week and today the nurse prescriber is with them while they are helping to bath Ben. The nurse notices the baby has a mild nappy rash. She is keen to prescribe zinc and castor oil ointment but Chrissy and Alf want a prescription for E45 cream because they feel this works very well.

The family is likely to be well known to the nurse prescriber and assessment of the family's needs will be ongoing. The psychological and social circumstances have to be carefully considered in the potential prescribing situation, for example:

- the home and its facilities
- the nature of support services
- the abilities of the parents
- ways to both empower Chrissy and Alf, and to work towards prescribing a product that is safe and effective and will be used appropriately.

The scenario raises professional issues in respect of clinical decision-making. E45 cream can be prescribed but it is an emollient for dry skin conditions, not a barrier cream. The National Prescribing Centre (1999a, p. 3) notes:

> A prescribing decision may be viewed as a shared contract between patient and prescriber. This shared decision making is known as concordance.

Communication is essential; the nurse prescriber must listen carefully to Chrissy and Alf's arguments for their product preference. She has to present carefully and sensitively her own rationale, ensuring that it is fully understood.

The nurse prescriber is accountable for her actions and this involves prescribing that is safe and effective. Prescribing zinc and castor oil ointment is both, but if Chrissy and Alf do not accept the nurse's advice and fail to use the product it will be neither as Ben is left untreated. Prescribing E45 cream will be meeting the parents' needs; it is not unsafe but neither is it likely to be effective in treating the nappy rash. It may be useful to explore other barrier cream options so that the prescriber and the parents feel confident in the product and its use.

Case study 7

Hilary Gordon has twins of three years and a six-month-old baby. She works part-time at the local supermarket and tells the nurse prescriber that she is always tired. She is still breastfeeding baby Rod three or four times a day including during the night. Hilary says she has experienced frequent headaches in the last couple of weeks. She thinks this is partly due to her tiredness but also to tension because of some financial worries. In addition she knows that she is not sitting comfortably when on the checkout at work and that she often has backache and neck stiffness. She has taken nothing for the aches and pains fearing that any medication would pass into the breast milk and adversely affect Rod.

That Hilary is tired would not seem surprising given the circumstances, however minor aches and pains can exacerbate these feelings and a mild pain relief would be appropriate. An interesting dimension in respect of nurse prescribing is whether to prescribe paracetamol or recommend Hilary buy the product. As she works at a supermarket it will be easy for her to purchase the product cheaply if she buys it under the generic name rather than a proprietary brand. Reassurance that the baby will experience no adverse affects should give her confidence in the proposed pain management. Possible advantages of prescribing however include the psychological comfort that may come from having the nurse prescriber treat the problem. Moreover, it may be some time before she next goes to work and this will delay the treatment; a nurse prescription will ensure treatment is started promptly. Whatever the decision, the nurse prescriber has a duty to give accompanying health information in respect of dosage and the dangers of overdose. As there are young children in the household the importance of safe storage needs to be properly explored. Accompanying health education should be incorporated into the care, for example the benefits of localised pain relief such as warm baths or relaxation techniques, social support, contact with the occupational health department.

Case study 8

Helen, aged 44, has multiple sclerosis and has been wheelchair bound for two years. She has recently been in respite care while her mother, who is the main carer, had a holiday. During a home visit, Helen informs the nurse that she has developed a small pressure sore on her left heel.

Clark (1999) divides factors relating to pressure sore formation into three groups. Extrinsic factors, that is, mechanical forces of pressure, shear and friction, intrinsic factors such as those that reduce the skin's resistance to mechanical damage, for example immobility, malnourishment, underlying pathology, and so on and external factors which relate to carer interactions. These could include infrequent or inappropriate repositioning, poor lifting technique and poor hygiene where the skin is under attack from excessive moisture. A full assessment is necessary to identify the type and severity of the pressure sore, and to facilitate this a grading system, which describes sore severity by depth, could be used. According to Kingsley and Murray (1999), adoption of a single grading system within a locality aids communication across the whole care team, providing documentary evidence of assessment and a means to describe deterioration or improvement. The nurse prescriber should therefore utilise any local guidance relating to wound assessment as appropriate.

Wound assessment should include location of wound, form, aetiology, tissue type, size, whether exudate is present, pain assessment and general skin condition. In the case of pressure sores, the pressure sore risk assessment score should be calculated (National Prescribing Centre 1999b). It is widely accepted that a warm, moist environment encourages healing and prevents tissue dehydration and cell death. Dressings that fulfil these requirements include foam and foam film dressings, hydrocolloids and hydrogels. The nurse should utilise his or her clinical judgement based on a careful and accurate assessment of Helen's general condition and her sore heel to prescribe the most appropriate dressing from the *Nurse Prescribers' Formulary* (NPF). Assessment and regular reassessment of wounds is essential in order to optimise wound management. Advice regarding diet, fluid intake and relief of pressure on the affected part should also be given.

Case study 9

Tim Biggins, aged 45 years, lives alone in a rented bedsit. He became known to Andy, a nurse prescriber, because of the health care that he provided to him 12 months ago. Tim was highly suspicious of the health services but Andy worked hard and built up a therapeutic relationship with Tim that was not only accepted but also appreciated.

Two weeks ago Tim sought Andy's advice on an unrelated health problem. The complaint was of sore and itchy skin on several parts of the body. An examination revealed burrows on his hands and feet and a distinctive symmetric rash around trunk and armpits. Suspecting scabies Andy sent a scraping to the laboratory. The results have returned, confirming the diagnosis.

This scenario provides a good example of how nurse prescribing may enhance aspects of nursing practice. The implication is that Tim may have refused to attend a doctor for care but clearly trusts the nurse, who can offer health education and prescribe appropriate treatment.

In this case the nurse opted to confirm diagnosis by sending a scraping to the laboratory, although the signs and symptoms themselves were highly indicative of scabies. As a new prescriber Andy was perhaps correct to be cautious; a more experienced practitioner is likely to be able to diagnose by observing the rash, including the burrows, and possibly the mite, as well as by taking a history from the patient.

The NPF offers the nurse prescriber two alternatives in treating scabies, malathion and permethrin. The former is available in lotion, the latter as cream. The former is left on for 24 hours, the latter for 8–12 hours. The other significant difference between the two is that the former is half the price of the latter. Within the current NHS philosophy of evidence-based practice, the prescribing dilemma concerning product choice for treating scabies is particularly noteworthy since there is an acknowledged lack of empirical evidence supporting one over the other (National Prescribing Centre 1999c). A recent systematic review carried out for the Cochrane Infectious Diseases Group is discussed in *Effectiveness Matters* (The University of York NHS Centre for Reviews and Dissemination 1999, p. 1) where it is stated:

> While permethrin appears to be the preferred treatment for scabies at the present time, this choice is based on small trials together with traditional reviews and professional opinion.

Griffiths (1999) argues that evidence-based health care is a challenge and suggests that nurses should fill any gaps with their own research or with opinion that is subjected to rigorous scrutiny.

As with all nurse prescribing situations the decision to prescribe or recommend the patient/client buy the product has to be taken. In this case cost may be significant and determining if Tim is employed; whether he is entitled to free prescriptions and whether he will spend money on appropriate treatment should be taken into account.

Case study 10

The nurse prescriber is visiting Anne-Louise and her 14-day-old baby Oliver. Oliver is Anne-Louise's first baby. He was a full-term forceps delivery.

Oliver appears to be a normal healthy infant, however the nurse prescriber notices that he has oral thrush. He is bottle feeding well and appears settled.

If the nurse prescriber is the health visitor, this is probably the first visit to the family following the birth of Oliver and a full health visiting assessment will be undertaken. Although the oral thrush requires treatment, it is important that the condition does not dominate the visit. Many of the assessment issues pertaining to the infection apply anyway, including aspects of feeding management, maternal health and social support. If the nurse prescriber is the community midwife she will already know the family and these factors are likely to have been assessed previously.

Courtney and Butler (1999) suggest that the commonest cause of candida albicans in the newborn is from maternal vaginal infection. It is prudent to determine if this may the case by taking a history from Anne-Louise. Other ways of the infant acquiring the infection are from contaminated hands, bottles and teats or other articles (Wong 1997, cited by Courtney and Butler 1999). Hygiene procedures should be discussed as usual with the necessary health education advice in respect of sterilisation of bottles and dummies. There are two alternatives in the 1999–2001 NPF for the treatment of oral thrush, miconazole oral gel and nystatin oral suspension. The expanded *Formulary* has the additional product amphotericin, although if the health visitor has not undertaken the further training to prescribe from the expanded

Formulary she will be unable to prescribe this. All treatments require application four times a day and must be continued for 48 hours after the lesions have resolved. It is important that sufficient medication is provided to allow this.

It is not uncommon for the infection to also be present in the nappy area, and the nurse prescriber should examine this. Anne-Louise needs to be informed of what to look for and to contact a health professional if a rash develops.

Case study 11

Maureen Harry lives with her three children aged 8, 7 and 6 years in a caravan on a local authority site for travelling families. The family has been resident for over a month but has only recently registered with a GP. Maureen attends the health centre because several children at the local school have head lice and she asks for a prescription for the children.

Head lice infestation represents a significant public health issue. Historically the condition was seen to have an association with uncleanness and unfortunately this myth prevails. The social stigma attached to the infestation may be contributing to some of the difficulties in effective treatment. Families are sometimes reluctant to inform contacts of head lice infestation, allowing further spread. It is also not uncommon to find children without head lice being 'treated' by the inappropriate use of insecticides. This may result in resistance of head lice to some products. In this case Maureen has merely heard of some children at the school being infested and treatment is inappropriate on this basis. Giving relevant health education in a sensitive manner is the major role of the nurse prescriber. Before insecticide treatment is started it is necessary for a live louse to be seen and Maureen needs to know exactly what she is looking for. In some health authorities there may be protocols in place noting that a live louse has to be seen by a health professional before a prescription is given. Other area protocols allow for the presentation of a specimen by the client. The obvious disadvantage is that it may not be from the head of the person for whom the prescriber writes the prescription. Many nurse prescribers may incorporate a head check as part of the assessment and the nurse may offer to look at Maureen's head there and then. The prescribing nurse could invite Maureen to bring the children to the health centre after school so they too may be assessed. Only the people infested (if any) should be treated but it may be pertinent to discuss the possible benefits of 'bug-busting', the procedure where wet, conditioned hair is methodically combed with a fine tooth comb. The benefits of this procedure in detecting and treating headlice are currently under systematic review, since no reliable evidence exists confirming or refuting success. However, small scale audits of community initiatives using the method seem to have been beneficial (Duncan 1997; Fee et al. 2000), although whether this was due to the procedure or to the other health promoting activities that accompanied the campaigns is unclear.

Case study 12

Jean calls into the health centre for advice about her two children, John aged 5 years and David aged 10 years, who have been complaining of a distressing peri-anal itch for the past week. The children are becoming tired and irritable. This morning Jean examined both children carefully and noticed small (8–12 mm) threadlike worms in the peri-anal area. She tells the nurse prescriber that both children are red and sore in this area.

Unlike treatments for headlice it is recommended that the whole family be treated for threadworms whether symptomatic or not since reinfection is common. The drug of choice for patients over two years is mebendazole, which is available as oral suspension or tablets. Usually one dose is all that is necessary although as reinfection is possible a second dose two-to-three weeks later may be given. The tablets are available in pack sizes of six but an important prescribing point here is that the nurse must write a separate prescription for each member of the family. Health education advice is essential in respect of hand washing and general hygiene procedures. A cream to ease the peri-anal itching will assist in breaking the cycle of autoinfection.

During the assessment Jean informs the nurse prescriber that she is two days late with her menstrual period and this morning she did a home pregnancy test that confirmed her suspicion that she is pregnant. Having considered her family complete, this has come as a shock; nevertheless she is pleased by the news.

This aspect of the scenario highlights the significance of the prescribing assessment. The NPF states that the nurse prescriber should not prescribe any medicine at all to a patient who is pregnant; Jean should be referred to the GP. The use of both mebendazole and piperazine are cautioned in pregnancy. Strict hygiene procedures will eradicate the cycle of autoinfection and this is likely to be the advice choice of the GP. However, a caution is not the same as a contraindication and the nurse prescriber must not instil unnecessary anxieties into the patient in case a prescription is deemed necessary by the GP.

A further prescribing issue raised by the pregnancy concerns folic acid, which is advised for the prevention of neural tube defects. The nurse can prescribe this and Jean should be recommended to start the supplement at once and continue until the twelfth week of pregnancy.

Case study 13

The nurse has been asked to make a home visit to Mrs Cordingley, aged 82 years, who lives alone in a warden-controlled flat. She is incontinent of urine and has decreased mobility due to osteoarthritis. Frequent contact with urine has caused the skin of her groins and buttocks to become increasingly excoriated. To prevent any further deterioration, the GP has suggested that insertion of an indwelling catheter may help to alleviate the problem giving Mrs Cordingley's skin a chance to heal. Intermittent catheterisation is not thought to be an appropriate option in this case.

According to Pomfret (2000), approximately 12 per cent of hospital patients and 4 per cent of community-based patients have an indwelling catheter for a wide variety of reasons. This scenario highlights the need for a holistic approach, as use of a catheter entails a significant lifestyle adjustment on the part of the patient and it is important that nurses play an active role in educating patients and involving them in the decision-making process (Doherty 2001). Empowerment and knowledge of their condition can ensure greater concordance with care plans and help patients avoid the problems associated with indwelling urethral or suprapubic catheters. The nurse prescriber should undertake a full assessment prior to catheterisation and relevant information regarding types of catheter, appropriate drainage bags, bag supports, and so on should be discussed with Mrs Cordingley. General health advice should also be given to the patient. This should include advice about diet and maintaining fluid intake, avoiding constipation, and advice regarding personal hygiene especially round the genital area.

Regarding the skin excoriation, the nurse would need to assess the extent and type of rash, whether any barrier cream has already been prescribed by the GP and if so, if it is being used appropriately. Le Lievre (2001) indicates that little research is available on barrier products although she does suggest a zinc oxide ointment for skin that is severely irritated. In this situation, ideally the catheter should be for short- to medium-term use only (National Prescribing Centre 1999d; Le Lievre 2001). Regular review and planned follow-up are essential to ensure products prescribed are both effective and acceptable to the patient. Nurses should be guided by local formularies and guidelines that are regularly updated (National Prescribing Centre 1999b) although, as noted by Le Lievre (2001, p. 183), 'treatment protocols are varied and are not always supported by evidence'. This gives prescribing nurses opportunity for audit and a role in the development of future protocols based on best practice.

References

Aronson, E. (1980) *The Social Animal* (3rd edn). W.H. Freeman and Co., San Francisco.

Blenkinsop, A. and Paxton, P. (1998) *Symptoms in the Pharmacy. A Guide to the Management of Common Illness* (3rd edn). Blackwell, Oxford.

Clark, C .(1999) The problem of pressure sores and how to treat them. *Hospital Magazine*, March: 8–13.

Courtney, M. and Butler, M. (1999) *Nurse Prescribing Principles and Practice*. Greenwich Medical Media, London.

Doherty,W. (2001) Promoting planned care for patients with indwelling catheters. *British Journal of Community Nursing*, 6(1): 11–16.

Duncan, C. (1997) Bug busters. *Nursing Times*, 93(49): 46–7.

Fee, J., Briault, V. and Long, J. (2000) A community approach to reducing headlice infection. *Community Practitioner*, 73(2): 477–80.

Glossop, C. (1996) Perineal care after childbirth. *Health Visitor,* 69(3): 96–9.

Griffiths, P. (1999) The challenge of implementing evidence-based health care. *British Journal of Community Nursing,* 4(3): 142–7.

Hallett, C.E., Austin, L., Caress, A. and Luker, K.A. (2000) Wound care in the community setting clinical decision making in context. *Journal of Advanced Nursing,* 31(4): 783–93.

Kingsley, A. and Murray, J. (1999) Prevention and management of pressure sores in the community. *Primary Health Care,* 9: (6).

Landsell-Smith, J. (2001) Diagnosis and management of fungal infections of the skin. *British Journal of Community Nursing,* 6(4): 186–92.

Le Lievre, S. (2001) The management and prevention of incontinence dermatitis. *British Journal of Community Nursing,* 6(4): 180–5.

Lipley, N (2000) Rich pickings. *Nursing Standard,* 14(36): 12–13.

Magee, P. (2000) The pharmaceutical rep – to see or not to see. *Primary Health Care,* 10(7): 33–4.

National Prescribing Centre (1999a) Signposts for prescribing nurses – general principles of good prescribing. *Prescribing Nurse Bulletin,* 1(1).

National Prescribing Centre (1999b) Modern wound management dressings. *Prescribing Nurse Bulletin,* 1(2).

National Prescribing Centre (1999c) The management of scabies and threadworms. *Prescribing Nurse Bulletin,* 1(3).

National Prescribing Centre (1999d) Prescribing in urinary incontinence. *Prescribing Nurse Bulletin,* 1(5).

NHS Executive (1998) *Nurse Prescribing. A Guide for Implementation.* NHSE, Leeds, December.

Pomfret, I. (2000) Urinary catheters: selection, management and prevention of infection. *British Journal of Community Nursing,* 5: 6–13.

Sleep, J. and Grant, A. (1988) Relief of perineal pain after childbirth: a survey of midwifery practice. *Midwifery,* 4(3): 118–22.

Steen, M. and Cooper, K. (1998) Cold therapy and perineal wounds: too cool or not too cool? *British Journal of Midwifery,* 6(9): 572–9.

The University of York NHS Centre for Reviews and Dissemination (1999) Treating headlice and scabies. *Effectiveness Matters,* 4(1).

UKCC (1992) *Code of Professional Conduct.* UKCC, London.

Young, F (2001) Management of genital thrush. *Professional Care of Mother and Child,* 11(1): 12–14.

11

Nurse prescribing: the future

Jennifer L. Humphries and Joyce Green

This final chapter of the book will look forward to examine nurse prescribing as it increasingly becomes part of nursing practice for many nurses working in a variety of roles and settings.

Current developments in nurse prescribing

The NHS Plan, published in July 2000, signifies a reform of health-care changes throughout the NHS. While the ethos is based on the needs and wants of patients and potential patients (that is, the public) there is obvious evidence that NHS staff, including nurses, are vital to the success of the plan. The publication *Investment and Reform for NHS Staff – Taking Forward the NHS Plan* (DoH 2001a) is clear that, while increasing the numbers of nurses is impor-tant, working in new ways is essential to the successful delivery of the changes. Nurse prescribing has first mention in the chapter about changing the way staff work, with commitment to extending nurse prescribing, supporting the declaration in *Making a Differ-ence* (DoH 1999a, p. 12) that, 'Nurse prescribing is here to stay'.

In May 2001, Health Minister Lord Philip Hunt provided further detail when he announced an expansion of nurse prescribing (DoH 2001b). Two significant elements to nurse prescribing were announced, the first concerned the development of prescribing to include further groups of nurses; the second declared the intention to expand the NPF (see Appendix 2 for proposed list).

Between 2002 and 2004 10,000 nurses will be trained and be able to prescribe from this expanded *Formulary* and it seems inevitable that, as benefits to patient care continue to manifest, the next groups of prescribing nurses will simply be the first of many more. As Baroness Cumberlege notes in the Foreword to the first edition of this book, nurse prescribing is 'unstoppable'.

Certain nurses working in areas of palliative care and health promotion and some of those involved in nurse-led clinical situations will become the next generation of nurse prescribers. These prescribing nurses will be able to prescribe from a far more extensive *Nurses' Formulary* than that currently available for district nurse and health visitor prescribers, and for a broader range of medical conditions, under the treatment areas of minor injuries, minor ailments, health promotion and palliative care.

A further option for nurses in the future is the prospect of becoming supplementary prescribers. Nurse practitioners and nurses with a specialist role, for example those caring for patients with complex or chronic disease including coronary heart disease and hypertension and those such as stoma therapists, diabetic and asthma specialist nurses, and specialist practitioners in mental health, are likely to be given the opportunity to become supplementary prescribers. This is broadly in line with the recommendations from the Crown Report (DoH 1999b) where two categories of prescriber were identified; the independent prescriber who:

> takes responsibility for the clinical assessment of the patient (usually establishing a diagnosis) as well as for the appropriateness of any prescription which may be issued at that time
>
> (p. 37)

and the dependent prescriber who is responsible for the care of the patient after initial assessment and diagnosis by a clinician.

Whether an independent or a supplementary prescriber a nurse is responsible for the episode of care she or he provides including any medication she or he prescribes. Several factors must be met: first, the nurse must be qualified and expert in the role she or he is currently undertaking; second, appropriate education and training must be available to ensure that the nurse is confident and competent in the ability to prescribe, both initially and also in continuing professional development; third, the nurse must integrate the new element of practice into the existing role.

Expansion of the *Nurse Prescribers' Formulary*

The expansion of the *Nurse Prescribers' Formulary* is welcome news although some may feel that the changes have not gone far enough, that it is a compromise and a 'missed opportunity' (Lipley 2001). Others are more pragmatic feeling that, while the reform is limited, it is a significant step and one that can be built on (O'Dowd 2001). The 'second generation' of nurse prescribers will, after training, be able to prescribe general sales list and pharmacy medicines, which are prescribable by doctors under the NHS, together with a list of prescription-only medicines (POMs), linked to specific medical conditions.

In many nursing situations the range of products that is available under general sales list and pharmacy medicines will meet prescribing treatment for patients or clients. In addition the 12 POMs in the 1999–2001 NPF are already included in Schedule 3 of POM Order and may also be prescribed. Advice was taken from the Committee on Safety of Medicines concerning additional POMs that may be required to treat such medical conditions as:

- Acne
- Bacterial vaginosis
- Blepharitis
- Candida infection of the mouth, skin and vulvovagina
- Chronic skin ulcer
- Colds and sore throat
- Constipation
- Conjunctivitis
- Cental abscess
- Eczema
- Furuncle
- Gastroenteritis
- Gingivitis
- Haemorrhoids
- Heartburn
- Herpes
- Impetigo
- Lower urinary tract infection (uncomplicated)
- Mouth ulcer
- Otitis externa and media
- Rhinitis and sinusitis
- Ringworm
- Seborrhoeic dermatitis

- Sprains and strains
- Superficial phlebitis
- Threadworms

(MCA 2001)

Other POMs suggested for prescribing by nurses are:

- A selection of oral antibiotics that may be used to treat the above conditions.
- A selection of analgesics and non-steroidal anti-inflammatory drugs.
- A range of products for contraceptive management including the pill, injectable contraceptives, intrauterine devices, diaphragms, spermicides and emergency contraception.
- A range of routine childhood and specific vaccinations.
- A range of drugs often used in palliative care, for example treatments for anorexia, cough, dry mouth, excessive respiratory secretions, fatigue, hiccup, nausea and vomiting, restlessness and confusion, pain control.

(MCA 2001)

The full list of medical conditions and the prescription-only medicines proposed by the MCA may be found on the MCA website at www.mca.gov.uk.

The additional POMs list proposed by the Medicines Control Agency (see Appendix 2) was subject to wide consultation before the *Formulary* was finalised. To some extent the exact nature of the NPF is incidental since whatever nurses prescribe the vital point is that they are competent to do so, a feature common to all aspects of care provided by nurses. Many of the principles employed in delivering care that includes issuing a prescription apply, no matter what is prescribed. The seven principles of good prescribing outlined by the National Prescribing Centre (1999) suggest these should be:

1. Examine the holistic needs of the patient. Is a prescription necessary?
2. Consider the appropriate strategy.
3. Consider the choice of product.
4. Negotiate a 'contract' and achieve concordance with the patient/client.
5. Review the patient on a regular basis.
6. Ensure record keeping is both accurate and up to date.
7. Reflect on prescribing.

Nevertheless an increased number of prescribable products will clearly have implications in terms of nurses' theoretical knowledge of pharmacology and may raise issues pertaining to diagnostic skills and clinical decision-making. A national survey commissioned by the ENB (Latter et al. 2001) to evaluate nurses' educational preparation for, and practice of, medication education showed that both pre- and post-registration respondents on nurse education programmes considered that insufficient time in the curriculum was dedicated to pharmacology.

Education and training

From 2002 there will be two types of preparation for certain nurses to become prescribers. The existing training of district nurse and health visitor students as prescribers remains as part of the community specialist practitioner course and these practitioners will continue to prescribe from the current NPF, which although quite limited is focused on their particular roles (see Appendix 1). For the new generation nurse prescriber with the expanded *Formulary* a completely new educational preparation programme has been developed by the ENB (2001) for course delivery at Higher Education Institutions.

Entrants to the nurse prescribing education programme must:

- Be first level nurses, from any part of the register. At the present time it will not be open to second level nurses.
- Have appropriate experience in the area of practice in which they will be prescribing.
- Have the ability to study at academic level III.
- Have support from the employing organisation.
- Have a designated medical practitioner who will provide the supervision, support and shadowing opportunities to develop competence in prescribing practice.

(ENB 2001)

Clearly the educational preparation for nurse prescribers has to be robust. It is vital that nurses are adequately prepared for the responsibility of adding a new element to their role and the education and training required to enable nurses to prescribe safely and effectively must continue to be carefully monitored. It would also seem prudent that pre-registration courses incorporate more pharmacology that will prepare nurses for specialist roles in the future.

The UKCC (1999a) recommendations for pre-registration education have been influenced by the changing professional role of the nurse, of which prescribing is just one example. In an earlier document the UKCC (1999b) noted that:

> It is reasonable to assume that the role developments already seen in nursing, midwifery and health visiting are likely to continue. These changes have increased the skills and decision-making capacity of all practitioners. Continuing changes in the structure, funding and organisation of health care in all settings will continue to offer challenging new roles and opportunities for all nurses, midwives and health visitors.
>
> (p. 30)

There are numerous nurses with very specialist skills in many areas of practice, for example in cardiology, renal nursing and palliative care. The increasing range and complexity of roles undertaken by nurses has to be supported by proper education and training and nurse prescribing is no exception. The consultation paper (DoH 2000) notes that the preparation for nurses to prescribe from an expanded *Formulary* will be a key factor in ensuring safe, clinically effective and cost-effective prescribing. Prescribing encompasses a range of skills within cognitive (knowledge), affective (attitudes and values) and psychomotor (motor skills) domains of learning (Quinn 1995) and the preparation courses must reflect this and be of high quality.

The training will be at academic level III with a taught programme of 25 days and 12 days' practice delivered over a 3-month period. A medical practitioner will provide the nurse with shadowing opportunities, supervision and support during the practice element of the course and will also serve as assessor. A range of assessment strategies will be employed to determine knowledge, decision-making and the application of theory to practice (ENB 2001). In addition to the assessment of practice, students will also undertake a clinical examination, a written examination and a review of a portfolio or learning log completed during the course.

Scope of Professional Practice

The intention of the *Scope of Professional Practice* (UKCC 1992a) is to encourage nurses to develop their skills and expertise in relation to their own situation, for example their clinical area, and their decision to learn is to meet the needs of patients or clients within that area. Whether nurse prescribing is an extension or an expansion of nurses' roles is a moot point. Extension of role implies that nurses are undertaking tasks or procedures not normally part of existing practice. Conversely expanding a role suggests the incorporation of additional skills and/or knowledge that develop and enhance an existing role. The *Scope of Professional Practice* (UKCC 1992a) favours the latter term because it emphasises the practitioner's decision to learn within their own sphere of practice in order to meet the needs of clients and patients.

The 23,000 or so community nurses and health visitors who were prescribers at the end of the national roll-out of the initiative in April 2001 had no choice in undertaking the training. Moreover, all students beginning the community specialist practitioner course to become a district nurse or health visitor have nurse prescribing automatically incorporated and thus prescribing is as much a part of the role as, say, venepuncture or child protection.

With the continuing development of nurse prescribing the approach is more flexible so that nurses become prescribers according to the needs of their role and the context in which they work. It will be dependent on the employer to determine where nurse prescribing will benefit patients. Successful completion of a programme that qualifies a nurse to prescribe will not automatically entitle him or her to do so. Employers will identify those posts where nurse prescribing will most benefit patients.

Prescribing adds a further dimension to existing practice and compels nurse prescribers to recognise their own level of competence and decline duties for which they do not feel prepared. This is not an unusual phenomenon in prescribing. A GP from the evaluation study by Luker et al. (1997c) noted that, although he had the potential to prescribe from the whole of the *British National Formulary* (BNF), he clearly would not do so if he did not feel competent. He continues, regarding nurse prescribing, 'I am aware that this system is already operative because the health visitors do not prescribe dressing packs because it is not within their sphere of work' (p. 37).

Continuing professional development

The legal capacity to prescribe offers an additional option for nurses in the delivery of patient care but just because a nurse can prescribe does not mean she or he will always do so. Referral to a doctor will continue to be a significant alternative for any nurse prescriber. Even with the proposed expansion, the NPF is limited in the number of preparations available on a nurse prescription and thus a prescribing nurse may have to refer to a medical colleague if a patient requires a product not available. Nurses must also be aware of their own restrictions: the ability to acknowledge a lack of knowledge with which to make a diagnosis is a competent recognition of personal or professional limitations; it is not an admission of ineptitude. Nonetheless the practitioner and the employer must be confident that the practitioner has the skills and knowledge to fulfil his or her role effectively, taking the *Scope of Professional Practice* (UKCC 1992a) and the *Code of Professional Conduct* (UKCC 1992b) into account (Wallace 1998). According to the UKCC (2000), the *Scope of Professional Practice* has a positive role to play in the delivery of the care by nurses, midwives and health visitors. It provides a framework for practitioners so they can:

> justify what they are able to do in order to ensure the effective delivery of care (and) identify what they are not in a position to do, due to lack of skills or knowledge, and how that might be remedied.
>
> (UKCC 2000, p. 4)

It is vital that nurses continuously evaluate their expertise in prescribing in the context of their own field of practice, case-load/workload and the products available in the NPF. They have a professional responsibility to ensure that their practice is up to date and, along with their employer, have a duty to ensure that any deficiencies in knowledge and skills are rectified. As Teasdale (2001, p. S7) notes, 'patients need to be assured that the professionals who deliver their care are up to date with the best evidence-based practice in their chosen speciality.' Where prescribing is concerned it is not something that can be left to chance or to the individual without support from employers. The National Prescribing Centre (NPC) is committed to ensuring that all prescribers (not just nurses) continue with their professional development and have produced a framework to help nurses maintain competency in prescribing (NPC 2001).

Patient group directions

One of the most controversial and confusing issues associated with nurse prescribing when first launched was the widespread use of group protocols that allowed nurses to administer medication without an individual having a prescription. The legality of the practice came under scrutiny and nurses working with group protocols welcomed the publication of the interim Crown review at the end of April 1998 (DoH 1998) when much of the uncertainty surrounding the usage of these protocols was lifted. The position was clarified further in March 2000 when the Medicines Control Agency (MCA 2000) produced a consultation document, changing the term to patient group directions (PGD) the proposals of which would:

> ensure that nurses and other health professionals who supply or administer medicines under such directions are acting within the law and that all patient group directions complied with specific legal criteria.
>
> (MCA 2000, para 1)

> A patient group direction is a specific written instruction for the supply and administration, or administration of a named medicine in an identified clinical situation. It applies to groups of patients who may not be individually identified before presenting for treatment. Patient group directions are drawn up locally by doctors, pharmacists and other health professionals, signed by a doctor or dentist, as appropriate and approved by an appropriate healthcare body.
>
> (MCA 2000, para 5)

Guidance for information that each PGD should contain is available on the DoH web site at http://www.doh.gov.uk/coinh.htm. Examples of PGDs and a flowchart to help determine if a PGD is appropriate for a particular clinical situation can be found at http://www.groupprotocols.org.uk.

There are many nurses who supply and administer named medicines in specific clinical situations by way of a patient group direction and for a significant number of these nurses becoming an independent nurse prescriber is unlikely to be necessary. This type of management works well in several primary and secondary care settings although the majority of patients will continue to receive medicines on an individual basis.

Further issues for consideration

Prescribing is still a relatively new venture for nurses in the UK and there will naturally be questions and concerns from members of the profession. The pioneers of the nurse prescribing initiative did not enter into the venture lightly. In an interview in 1996, Baroness Cumberlege said:

> My great passion has been nurse prescribing, I have been with it for ten years and I am determined it will succeed. But I have to be very careful that it doesn't fall apart, which it might if we haven't got the proper systems in place; if we haven't got the appropriate training; if the formulary is wrong; or if nurses actually feel inadequate. I would rather build on solid foundations and see the scheme succeed.

(Williams 1996, p. 22)

The nurse prescribing pilot was evaluated by a highly qualified and competent team led by Professor Karen Luker, a renowned expert in the fields of both community nursing and research. Clearly the DoH was comfortable with the results of the pilot and demonstration nurse prescribing initiatives, a feature which no doubt served to reassure the country's district nursing and health visiting professions that the benefits of their prescribing were in the best interests of their patients and their own professional practice.

Nonetheless, change of any description can cause anxiety, and while there are many nurses who will embrace the venture whole-heartedly, there are bound to be those with reservations. Some of the now-qualified nurse prescribers had more than the natural concerns that might be expected to occur with any new professional undertaking (Campbell and Collins 2001). The training is intended to equip nurses with the knowledge and skills necessary to be able to prescribe from the NPF. Practical and theoretical education goes a long way to assuaging anxieties, although the original prescribers deserve recognition for taking the nursing profession forward into an unknown arena.

In addition to the evaluation study conducted by Luker et al. (1997a), the nursing press has published information about how nurses are faring in their role as prescribers (Alderman 1996; Smith 1996; Winstanley 1996; Blatt 1997; Carlisle 1997; Clarke 2001). The overwhelming view is positive, suggesting that, for these early prescribers, prescribing in practice appears to have caused little anxiety. Early indications are that patients too, are in favour of nurses prescribing (Luker et al. 1997b, 1998; Brooks et al. 2001) and that it is cost-effective (Prescribing Support Unit 2000). Evidence from current prescribers suggests that the ability to prescribe a wider range of products than those available in the 1999–2001 NPF (Appendix 1) will continue to enhance patient care and enable the benefits of nurse prescribing to be realised further (Luker et al. 1997b; Prescribing Support Unit 2000; Humphries and Green 2001). With the expansion of the NPF the potential for nurses to make a significant difference to patient care will be realised in a variety of situations. Having nurses prescribe is particularly likely to benefit those patients living in or attending settings that are nurse-led, such as NHS walk-in centres, family planning clinics, accident and emergency and minor injury units, disease management clinics, nursing homes, hospices, community drop-in clinics and well person clinics.

As more nurses become prescribers, they have additional support in colleagues who are already prescribing, and, as the programme rolls out to involve more of the profession, it would seem pertinent to formalise this provision. It is likely that, with an increasing number of nurse prescribers, concerns will lessen as practitioners become familiar with the role before becoming prescribers themselves.

Clearly, the nursing profession cannot be complacent; those with misgivings about nurse prescribing undoubtedly have genuine reasons for their apprehension. It would not be prudent to dismiss these, and even staunch proponents of the scheme would do well to listen and respond to any uncertainties that appear. Since the notion of nurses taking on the prescribing role formally was first documented, there have been some reservations about the knowledge and expertise that nurses possess. The proposed expansion of the NPF and the extension of prescribing rights to a wider range of nurses exposes the profession to more scepticism about the ability and motives to prescribe. So far, little evidence is available to indicate the level or type of doubt that exists within nursing. This may be because many nurses not directly involved with the project have only slight information on which to base an informed argument. Moreover, reading about nurse prescribing is not the same as practising as a prescriber. In addition the generally positive atmosphere that surrounds nurse prescribing can perhaps deter those unsure of its benefits from venturing a less favourable opinion. Those of us convinced of the benefits for the nursing profession, and importantly for patient and client care, must create a climate in which honest opinion can be aired. There is a clear need for regular evaluation and the reporting of both positive and not so positive issues that arise within the arena of nurse prescribing. While anecdotal information is useful, the importance of properly structured and organised research within nurse prescribing practice cannot be overestimated.

Conclusion

Prescribing represents a significant development in nursing history. The extension of the authority to prescribe to a wide range of nurses along with the expansion of the NPF is a major step in allowing many nurses to provide a more comprehensive package of care for patients and clients. As more nurses take on the responsibility of prescribing it is apparent that training will need to be considered, both in pre-registration and post registration courses and in terms of continuing professional development. The vital prerequisite to nurse prescribing is that practitioners are competent to prescribe and feel confident to do so in order to enjoy this aspect of their role.

References

Alderman, C. (1996) Prescribing pioneers. *Nursing Standard*, **10**(18): 26–7.
Blatt, B. (1997) Nurse prescribing: are you ready? *Practice Nursing*, **8**(12): 11–13.

Brooks, N., Otway, C., Rashid, C., Kilty, L. and Maggs, C. (2001) Nurse Prescribing: what do patients think? *Nursing Standard*, 15(17): 33–8.
Campbell, P. and Collins, G. (2001) Prescribing for community nurses. *Nursing Times*, 97(28): 38–9.
Carlisle, D. (1997) Nurse prescribing wound dressings. *Nursing Times*, 93(28): 58–61.
Clarke, A. (2001) Peak practice. *Community Practitioner*, 74(2): 52.
DoH (1998) *Review of Prescribing, Supply and Administration of Medicines: A Report on the Supply and Administration Under Group Protocols*. DoH, London.
DoH (1999a) *Making a Difference*. DoH, London.
DoH (1999b) *Review of Prescribing, Supply and Administration of Medicines. Final Report*. DoH, London.
DoH (2000) *Consultation on Proposals to Extend Nurse Prescribing*. http://www.doh.gov.uk/nurseprescribing/index.htm.
DoH (2001a) *Investment and Reform for NHS Staff – Taking Forward the NHS Plan*. DoH, London.
DoH (2001b) *Patients to get quicker access to medicines*. Press release: reference 2001/0223. DoH, London.
ENB (2001) *Outline Curriculum for the Preparation of Nurses, Midwives and Health Visitors to Prescribe from the Extended Nurse Prescribers' Formulary*. ENB, London.
Gulland, A. (1998) The paperchase. *Nursing Times*, 94(17): 17.
Humphries, J. and Green, E. (2001) The Expansion of the Nurse Prescribers' Formulary. *Community Nurse*, 7(1): 27–33.
Latter, S., Rycroft-Malone, J., Yerrell, P. and Shaw, D. (2001) Nurses' educational preparation for a medication education role: findings from a national survey. *Nurse Education Today*, 21: 143–54.
Lipley, N. (2001) Prescribing compromise is 'missed opportunity'. *Nursing Standard*, 15(34): 4.
Luker, K.A., Austin, L., Hogg, C. et al. (1997a) Evaluation of Nurse Prescribing Final Report: Executive Summary. Unpublished report.
Luker, K.A., Austin, L., Willock, J., Ferguson, B. and Smith, K. (1997b) Patients' views of nurse prescribing. *Nursing Times*, 93(17) 51–4.
Luker, K.A., Austin, L., Hogg, C., Ferguson, B. and Smith, K. (1997c) Nurses' and GPs' views of the *Nurse Prescribers Formulary*. *Nursing Standard*, 11(22) 33–8.
Luker, K.A., Austin, L., Hogg, C., Ferguson, B. and Smith, K. (1998) Nurse–patient relationships: the context of nurse prescribing. *Journal of Advanced Nursing*, 28(2) 235–42.
Medicines Control Agency (2000) *Sale, Supply and Administration of Medicines by Health Professionals under Patient Group Directions*. MCA, London.
Medicines Control Agency (2001) Extended Prescribing of Prescription Only Medicines by Independent Nurse Prescribers. www.mca.gov.uk.
National Prescribing Centre (1999) Signposts for prescribing nurses – general principles of good prescribing. *Prescribing Nurse Bulletin*, 1(1).

National Prescribing Centre (2001) *Maintaining Competency in Prescribing: An Outline Framework to Help Nurse Prescribers.* NPC, Liverpool.

O'Dowd, A. (2001) Frustration at limit of reform. *Nursing Times,* 97(19): 4.

Prescribing Support Unit (2000) *Review of Nurse Prescribing 1997–2000.* Prescribing Support Unit, London.

Quinn, F.M. (1995) *The Principles and Practice of Nurse Education* (3rd edn). Chapman & Hall, London.

Smith, K. (1996) Prescriptions in a different hand. *Community Nurse,* 2(7): 8.

Teasdale, K. (2001) Lifelong learning, CPD and you. *Professional Nurse,* (Supplement) 16(8): S7.

UKCC (1992a) *Scope of Professional Practice.* UKCC, London.

UKCC (1992b) *Code of Professional Practice.* UKCC, London.

UKCC (1999a) *Fitness for Practice.* UKCC, London.

UKCC (1999b) *A Higher Level of Practice.* UKCC, London.

UKCC (2000) *Perceptions of the Scope of Professional Practice.* UKCC, London.

Wallace, M. (1998) Specialist practice: the transitional arrangements. *Nursing Times Learning Curve,* 2(4): 14–15.

Williams, K. (1996) Convinced of the cause. *Nursing Standard,* 10(23): 22–3.

Winstanley, F. (1996) Evaluation on site. *Primary Health Care,* 6(1): 11–12.

Appendix 1:
The *Nurse Prescribers'*
Formulary 1999–2001

The *Nurse Prescribers' Formulary* (NPF) forms an appendix to the *British National Formulary* (BNF). The products that nurses may prescribe are taken from 12 chapters of the BNF. The types of preparations that are included in the NPF are:

- laxatives
- analgesics
- local anaesthetics
- drugs for the mouth
- drugs for the removal of earwax
- drugs for threadworms
- drugs for scabies and head lice
- skin preparations
- agents for disinfection and cleansing
- wound management products
- elastic hosiery
- urinary catheters and appliances
- stoma care products
- appliances and reagents for diabetes
- fertility and gynaecological products
- nicotine replacement products (from May 2001)

Appendix 2:

Proposed List of Prescription Only Medicines for Prescribing by Independent Nurse Prescribers (Medicines Control Agency 2001 – Annex B of Consultation Letter MLX 273)

(www.mca.gov.uk)

From 2002 training and education will be available for nurses, midwives and health visitors to prescribe from the extended *Nurse Prescribers' Formulary*. In addition to being able to prescribe all general sales list and pharmacy medicines, which are prescribable by doctors under the NHS, they may also prescribe from a list of prescription-only medicines (POMs), linked to specific medical conditions. The Medicines Control Agency produced the following proposed list for consultation.

NB: The 12 POMs in the 1999–2001 NPF are already included in Schedule 3 of POM Order and may also be prescribed.

Proposed list of prescription-only medicines for prescribing by independent nurse prescribers

Drug	Use or administration and comments
Aciclovir	External
Acrivastine	Oral
Adapalene	External
Alclometasone dipropionate	External
Alimemazine tartrate (trimeprazine tartrate)	Oral
Amitriptyline hydrochloride	Palliative care – oral
Amorolfine hydrochloride	External
Amoxycillin trihydrate	Oral
Amphotericin	Local mouth treatment

Aspirin	Oral and rectal
Azelaic acid	External
Azelastine hydrochloride	Ophthalmic, nasal
Bacitracin zinc	Ophthalmic, external
Baclofen	Palliative care – oral
Beclometasone dipropionate	External, nasal
Betamethasone	External
Betamethasone dipropionate	External
Betamethasone sodium phosphate	Aural, nasal
Betamethasone valerate	External, rectal
Budesonide	Nasal
Carbamazepine	Palliative care – oral and rectal
Carbaryl	External
Carbenoxolone sodium	Mouthwash
Cefalexin (cephalexin)	Oral
Cetirizine hydrochloride	Oral
Chloramphenicol	Ophthalmic
Chlortetracycline hydrochloride	External, ophthalmic
Cimetidine	Oral
Cinchocaine hydrochloride	Rectal
Ciprofloxacin hydrochloride	Ophthalmic
Clindamycin phosphate	External, vaginal
Clobetasol propionate	External
Clobetasone butyrate	External
Clotrimazole	External
Codeine phosphate	Oral (CD – MDA Sch 5)
Co-Phenotrope	Oral (CD – MDA Sch 5)
Cyclizine	Palliative care – parenteral (oral is P)
Dantrolene sodium	Palliative care – oral
Desogestrel	Oral
Desoximetasone (Desoxymethasone)	External
Dexamethasone	Aural
Dexamethasone isonicotinate	Nasal
Diazepam	Palliative care – oral, parenteral and rectal (CD – MDA Sch 4)
Diclofenac diethylammonium	External
Diflucortolone valerate	External
Dihydrocodeine tartrate	Oral (CD – MDA Sch 5)
Domperidone	Palliative care – oral and rectal
Econazole	External
Econazole nitrate	Vaginal
Erythromycin	External
Erythromycin ethyl succinate	Oral
Erythromycin stearate	Oral
Ethinylestradiol	Oral
Etynodiol diacetate (ethynodiol diacetate)	Oral
Famotidine	Oral
Felbinac	External

Fenticonazole nitrate	Vaginal
Fexofenadine hydrochloride	Oral
Flucloxacillin sodium	Oral
Fluconazole	Oral
Fludroxycortide (Flurandrenolone)	External
Flumetasone pivalate	Aural
Flunisolide	Nasal
Fluocinolone acetonide	External
Fluocinonide	External
Fluocortolone hexanoate	External, rectal
Fluocortolone pivalate	External, rectal
Flurbiprofen	Lozenges
Fluticasone propionate	External, nasal
Framycetin sulphate	Ophthalmic
Fusidic acid	External, ophthalmic
Gabapentin	Palliative care – oral
Gentamicin sulphate	Aural, ophthalmic,
Gestodene	Oral
Gramicidin	Ophthalmic
Halcinonide	External
Hydrocortisone	External including rectal
Hydrocortisone acetate	External including rectal, aural
Hydrocortisone butyrate	External
Hydrocortisone sodium succinate	Lozenges
Hyoscine butylbromide	Palliative care – oral and parenteral
Hyoscine hydrobromide	Palliative care – oral, parenteral and transdermal
Ibuprofen	External, oral
Imipramine	Palliative care – oral
Ipratropium bromide	Nasal
Isotretinoin	External
Ketoconazole	External
Ketoprofen	External
Levocabastine hydrochloride	Nasal and ophthalmic
Levomepromazine (methotrimeprazine)	Palliative care – oral and parenteral
Levonorgestrel	Oral
Lithium succinate	External
Lodoxamide trometamol	Ophthalmic
Loperamide hydrochloride	Oral
Loratadine	Oral
Lorazepam	Palliative care – oral and parenteral (CD – MDA Sch 4)
Mebendazole	Oral
Medroxyprogesterone acetate	Injection
Mestranol	Oral
Metoclopramide hydrochloride	Palliative care – oral and parenteral
Metronidazole	External, oral, vaginal
Metronidazole benzoate	Oral

Miconazole	Dental lacquer, external
Miconazole nitrate	Vaginal
Midazolam	Palliative care – parenteral (CD – MDA Sch 4)
Mometasone furoate	External, nasal
Mupirocin calcium	External
Nedocromil sodium	Ophthalmic
Nefopan hydrochloride	Oral
Neomycin sulphate	External, ophthalmic and aural
Neomycin undecanoate	Aural
Nitrofurantoin	Oral
Nizatidine	Oral
Norethisterone	Oral
Norethisterone acetate	Oral
Norethisterone enanthate	Oral
Norgestimate	Oral
Norgestrel	Oral
Nystatin	External, local mouth treatment, vaginal
Ofloxacin	Ophthalmic
Oxytetracycline calcium	External
Oxytetracycline dihydrate	Oral
Oxytetracycline hydrochloride	External
Paracetamol	Oral
Penciclovir	External
Phenoxymethylpenicillin potassium	Oral
Piroxicam	External
Polymyxin B sulphate	Ophthalmic, external
Prednisolone hexanoate	Rectal
Prednisolone sodium phosphate	Aural
Ranitidine hydrochloride	Oral
Silver sulphadiazine	External
Sodium cromoglycate	Ophthalmic
Sodium valproate	Palliative care – oral and parenteral
Sulconazole nitrate	External
Terbinafine hydrochloride	External
Tetracycline hydrochloride	External
Tretinoin	External
Triamcinolone acetonide	Nasal, aural, oral paste, external
Trimethoprim	Ophthalmic, oral
Valproic acid	Palliative care – oral
Vaccine, Adsorbed Diptheria	Injection
Vaccine, Adsorbed Diptheria and Tetanus	Injection
Vaccine, Adsorbed Diptheria and Tetanus for Adults and Adolescents	Injection
Vaccine, Adsorbed Diptheria for Adults and Adolescents	Injection
Vaccine, Adsorbed Diptheria, Tetanus and Pertussis	Injection

Vaccine, BCG	Injection
Vaccine, BCG Percutaneous	Injection
Vaccine, Diptheria Toxoid,Tetanus Toxoid and Acellular Pertussis	Injection
Vaccine, Haemophilus Influenzae Type B (Hib)	Injection
Vaccine, Haemophilus Influenzae Type B (Hib) with Diptheria, Tetanus and Pertussis	Injection
Vaccine, Haemophilus Influenzae Type B, Diptheria, Tetanus and Pertussis	Injection
Vaccine, Hepatitis A	Injection
Vaccine, Hepatitis A With Typhoid	Injection
Vaccine, Hepatitis A, Inactivated, with Recombinant (DNA) Hepatitis B	Injection
Vaccine, Hepatitis B	Injection
Vaccine, Influenza	Injection
Vaccine, Live Measles, Mumps and Rubella (MMR)	Injection
Vaccine, Meningococcal Group C Conjugate	Injection
Vaccine, Meningococcal Polysaccharide A and C	Injection
Vaccine, Pneumococcal	Injection
Vaccine, Poliomyelitis, Inactivated	Injection
Vaccine, Poliomyelitis, Live (Oral)	Oral
Vaccine, Rubella, Live	Injection
Vaccine, Tetanus, Adsorbed	Injection
Vaccine, Typhoid, Live Attenuated (Oral)	Oral
Vaccine, Typhoid, Polysaccharide	Injection

The authors and publisher are grateful to the MCA for permission to include this proposed list.

Index

interactions 52–3, 74
prescriptions online 109
pricing, *see* drug pricing
records 22
reference sources 68–71
selected list 86–7
side-effects 73–4
side-effects, and non-compliance 100–1
testing for, in prisons 98
waste 91
see also medication/medicines; medicinal products; prescribing; prescriptions
Drug Tariff 69, 77
DUMP (Disposal of Unwanted Medicines) 91
duty of care 38

E
E45 cream 146
education and training
assessment strategies 7–8
community nurses 14
continuing professional development 163–4
English National Board (ENB) course for nurse prescribers 160–1
future planning 12–13, 14
learning outcomes 6
for nurse prescribers 4–8, 14, 91, 160–4, 165–6
Open Learning Pack 4, 6, 11, 28
patient education 48, 52
pharmacology 50, 160
postgraduate (GPs) 91
practice nurses 12–13
qualifications necessary for nurse prescribing 7, 131
Steering Group 5
taught course 3, 6–7
types of preparation 160
Working Group 5–6

emergencies, consent in 42
employers
accountability to 39
vicarious liability 42–3
English National Board for Nursing, Midwifery and Health Visiting (ENB) 3–4, 5
course for nurse prescribers 160–1
Open Learning Pack 4, 6, 11, 28
episiotomy pain, case study 142
ethics
accountability and 24–5
case studies 30–1
deontology *v.* utilitarianism 29, 30
ethical dilemmas 25, 28
ethical problems 25, 28
patients' interests 27–8
and prescribing issues 25–8, 29–30
and resource implications 27, 28, 29–30
theory and principles 23–30
ethnicity, and compliance 102–4, 106
evaluation, *see* assessment; nursing evaluation
evidence-based medicine 89–90
experience, and confidence 49–50
extensions to prescribing
Crown II report on 11, 93, 113
expansion of NPF 115, 138, 156, 158–60
to other groups of nurses 20, 34–5, 156–7
to other health professionals 11, 15, 93

F
Family Law Reform Act 1969 41
fatigue, case study 146–7
financial incentives
for compliance 105
in prescribing 87–8